SPANISH
PICTURE DICTIONARY

McGraw·Hill

New York   Chicago   San Francisco   Lisbon   London   Madrid   Mexico City
Milan   New Delhi   San Juan   Seoul   Singapore   Sydney   Toronto

Welcome to our picture dictionary!
Here's an exciting way for you to learn Spanish words and phrases that will help you talk about the world around you.
This dictionary is fun to use—look at all the things you can do:

I CAN SEE . . .
Spanish words that begin with A, or with PA, or with . .

COLORS AND SHAPES
Find the objects colored . . .
Are there any round objects?

SYLLABLES
Clap your hands as many times as the syllables of the words:
el co-jín; **la al-fom-bra**

TELLING THE DIFFERENCES
What is the difference between **el cepillo** and **el plumero**? What do they have in common?

DRAWINGS
Does **el ratón** have a tail? Does **la llave** have a hole?

SIZES
Which is the biggest object? And which is the smallest?

WHAT ARE THEY DOING?
Can you say what the baby is doing? And what about the girl?

In the living room
En el cuarto de estar

CEILING **EL TECHO**

CORNER **LA ESQUINA**

DOOR **LA PUERTA**

PAINTINGS **LOS CUADROS**

PORTRAIT **EL RETRATO**

LANDSCAPE **EL PAISAJE**

BLINDS **LA PERSIANA**

TELEVISION **EL TELEVISOR**

CUSHION **EL COJÍN**

IRONING BOARD **LA TABLA DE PLANCHAR**

BROOM **EL CEPILLO**

VACUUM **LA ASPIRADORA**

LAUNDRY BASKET **LA CESTA**

VASE **EL JARRÓN**

FRAME **EL MARCO**

CLOTH **EL TRAPO**

LAMP **LA LÁMPARA**

CANDLEHOLDER **EL CANDELABRO**

SEARCH AND FIND

Find all these things in the picture on the left.

You will notice that almost all the Spanish words in this book have **el**, **la**, **los**, or **las** before them. These words simply mean "the" and are usually used when you talk about things in Spanish.

At the back of this book you will find a Spanish-English Glossary and an English-Spanish Glossary, where you can look up words in alphabetical order and find out exactly where they are located in the book. There is also pronunciation help so that you can say each Spanish word correctly.

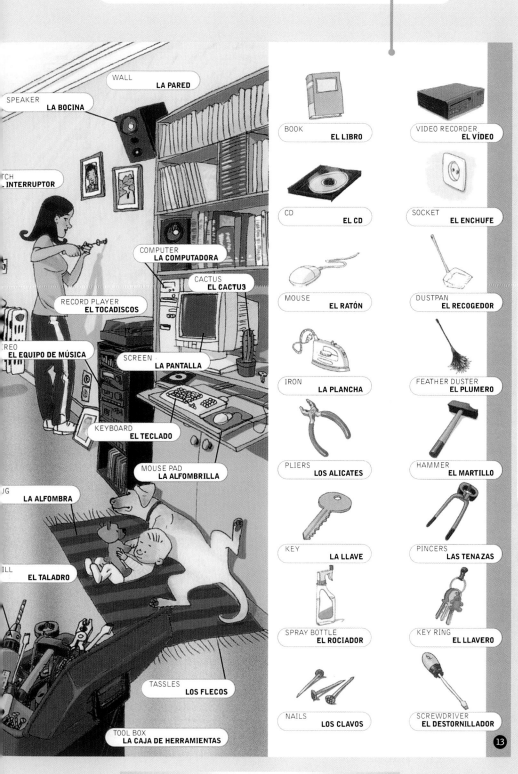

WALL — **LA PARED**
SPEAKER — **LA BOCINA**
TCH / .INTERRUPTOR
COMPUTER — **LA COMPUTADORA**
CACTUS — **EL CACTUS**
RECORD PLAYER — **EL TOCADISCOS**
REO — **EL EQUIPO DE MÚSICA**
SCREEN — **LA PANTALLA**
KEYBOARD — **EL TECLADO**
MOUSE PAD — **LA ALFOMBRILLA**
JG — **LA ALFOMBRA**
ILL — **EL TALADRO**
TASSLES — **LOS FLECOS**
TOOL BOX — **LA CAJA DE HERRAMIENTAS**

BOOK — **EL LIBRO**
CD — **EL CD**
MOUSE — **EL RATÓN**
IRON — **LA PLANCHA**
PLIERS — **LOS ALICATES**
KEY — **LA LLAVE**
SPRAY BOTTLE — **EL ROCIADOR**
NAILS — **LOS CLAVOS**

VIDEO RECORDER — **EL VÍDEO**
SOCKET — **EL ENCHUFE**
DUSTPAN — **EL RECOGEDOR**
FEATHER DUSTER — **EL PLUMERO**
HAMMER — **EL MARTILLO**
PINCERS — **LAS TENAZAS**
KEY RING — **EL LLAVERO**
SCREWDRIVER — **EL DESTORNILLADOR**

13

WHERE ARE THEY?

Is **el marco** near the girl? And who has **el destornillador**?

WHAT IS IT USED FOR?

What is **el teclado** used for?
What about **la aspiradora**?

McGraw-Hill's Spanish picture dictionary.
    96 p.: col. Ill.; 31 cm.
    ISBN 0-07-142812-7
    Includes glossaries.
    1. Picture dictionaries, Spanish—Juvenile literature.   2. Spanish language—Dictionaries, Juvenile—English.   3. Picture dictionaries, Spanish.   4. Picture dictionaries.   5. Spanish language materials—Bilingual.

PC4629 .I4313   2004
463'.21—dc22   2003061563

The **McGraw·Hill** Companies

Previously published under the original title: *IMAGINARIO. Diccionario en imágenes.* Copyright © Marcelo Pérez—Ediciones SM, 2001. All rights reserved. Published by arrangement with Ediciones SM.

ISBN 0-07-142812-7

TABLE OF CONTENTS • ÍNDICE DE MATERIAS

The family
La familia

ROLLER BLIND **EL ESTOR**

CLOCK **EL RELOJ**

BAG **LA BOLSA**

PRESENT **EL REGALO**

GRANDFATHER **EL ABUELO**

BALLOONS **LOS GLOBOS**

MOTHER **LA MADRE**

FATHER **EL PADRE**

SISTER **LA HERMANA**

BROTHER **EL HERMANO**

GRANDMOTHER **LA ABUELA**

PLANT **LA PLANTA**

BABY **EL BEBÉ**

UNCLE **EL TÍO**

CAKE **LA TORTA**

NAPKIN **LA SERVILLETA**

DRINKING STRAW **EL PITILLO**

PAPER STREAMER **LA SERPENTINA**

TABLECLOTH **EL MANTEL**

NEIGHBOR **EL VECINO**

AUNT **LA TÍA**

NEIGHBOR **LA VECINA**

COUSIN **EL PRIMO**

DOUGHNUT **LA ROSQUILLA**

CANDLE **LA VELA**

CHERRY **LA CEREZA**

MATCHES **LOS FÓSFOROS**

TOOTHPICKS **LOS PALILLOS**

MASK **LA CARETA**

CROWN **LA CORONA**

BOTTLE **LA BOTELLA**

GLASS **EL VASO**

ICE **EL HIELO**

SANDWICH **EL SÁNDWICH**

SANDWICH **EL BOCADILLO**

SALTSHAKER **EL SALERO**

NOISEMAKER **EL MATASUEGRAS**

PITCHER **LA JARRA**

HAIR **EL PELO**

POCKET **EL BOLSILLO**

RANGE HOOD
LA CAMPANA EXTRACTORA

MICROWAVE
EL MICROONDAS

SPICE RACK
EL ESPECIERO

SAUCEPAN
EL CAZO

CUTTING BOARD
LA TABLA PARA CORTAR

A PIECE OF TOAST
LA TOSTADA

JUICE
EL JUGO

OVEN
EL HORNO

JARS
LOS FRASCOS

BIB
EL BABERO

LID
LA TAPA

CEREAL
LOS CEREALES

HIGH CHAIR
LA TRONA

BOWL
EL TAZÓN

CARTON
EL CARTÓN

TRAY
LA BANDEJA

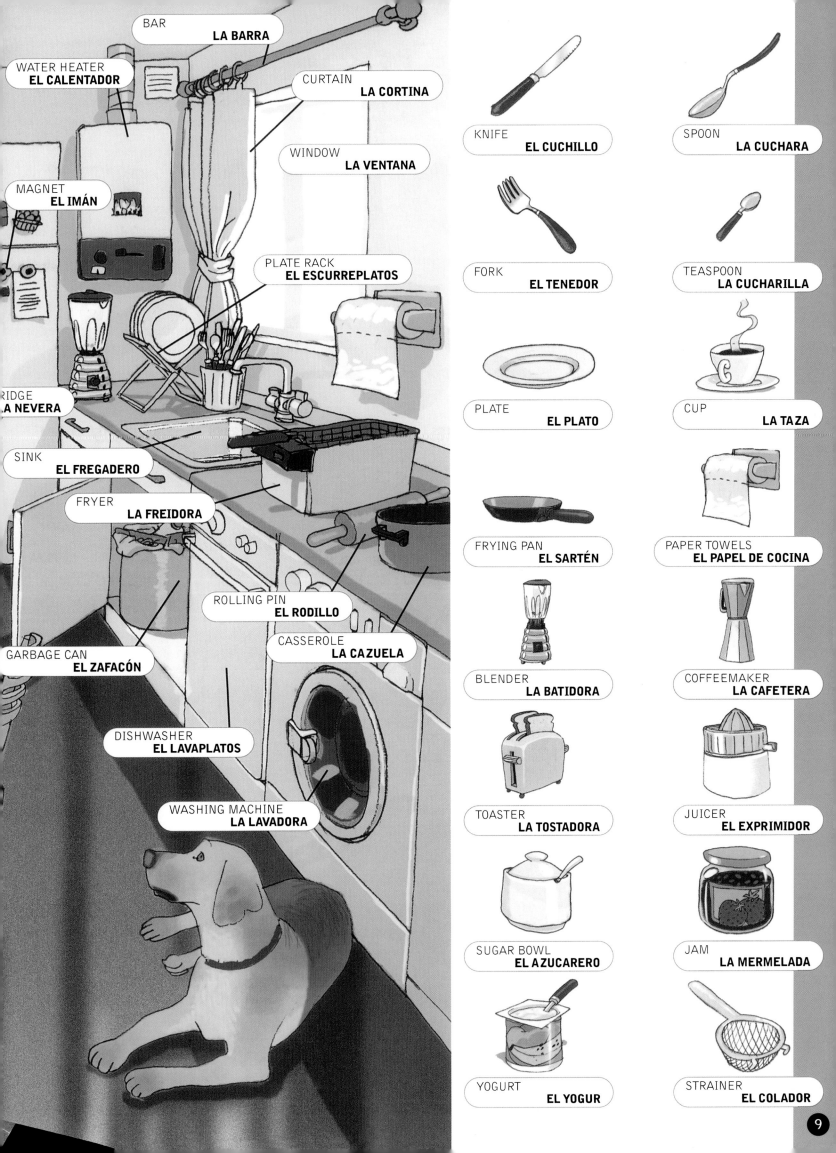

BAR
LA BARRA

WATER HEATER
EL CALENTADOR

CURTAIN
LA CORTINA

MAGNET
EL IMÁN

WINDOW
LA VENTANA

PLATE RACK
EL ESCURREPLATOS

RIDGE
A NEVERA

SINK
EL FREGADERO

FRYER
LA FREIDORA

ROLLING PIN
EL RODILLO

GARBAGE CAN
EL ZAFACÓN

CASSEROLE
LA CAZUELA

DISHWASHER
EL LAVAPLATOS

WASHING MACHINE
LA LAVADORA

KNIFE
EL CUCHILLO

SPOON
LA CUCHARA

FORK
EL TENEDOR

TEASPOON
LA CUCHARILLA

PLATE
EL PLATO

CUP
LA TAZA

FRYING PAN
EL SARTÉN

PAPER TOWELS
EL PAPEL DE COCINA

BLENDER
LA BATIDORA

COFFEEMAKER
LA CAFETERA

TOASTER
LA TOSTADORA

JUICER
EL EXPRIMIDOR

SUGAR BOWL
EL AZUCARERO

JAM
LA MERMELADA

YOGURT
EL YOGUR

STRAINER
EL COLADOR

Verduras y frutos

LETTUCE • **LA LECHUGA**

TOMATO • **EL TOMATE**

ONION • **LA CEBOLLA**

GARLIC • **EL AJO**

CARROT • **LA ZANAHORIA**

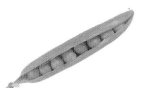

PEAS • **LOS GUISANTES**

BEANS • **LAS JUDÍAS VERDES**

ZUCCHINI • **EL CALABACÍN**

LEEK • **EL PUERRO**

TURNIP • **EL NABO**

POTATO • **LA PAPA**

CHARD • **LA ACELGAS**

ARTICHOKE • **LA ALCACHOFA**

PUMPKIN • **LA CALABAZA**

GREEN PEPPER •
EL PIMIENTO VERDE

RED PEPPER •
EL PIMIENTO ROJO

GREEN ASPARAGUS •
LOS ESPÁRRAGOS TRIGUEROS

WHITE ASPARAGUS •
LOS ESPÁRRAGOS BLANCOS

ALMONDS •
LAS ALMENDRAS

HAZELNUTS •
LAS AVELLANAS

PEANUTS •
LOS CACAHUETES

PISTACHIO NUTS •
LOS PISTACHOS

CASHEW NUTS •
LOS ANACARDOS

BANANA • **LA BANANA**

ORANGE • **LA NARANJA**

LEMON • **EL LIMÓN**

GRAPEFRUIT • **LA TORONJA**

APPLE • **LA MANZANA**

PEACH • **EL MELOCOTÓN**

APRICOT • **EL ALBARICOQUE**

MEDLAR • **EL NÍSPERO**

PEAR • **LA PERA**

MANGO • **EL MANGO**

AVOCADO • **EL AGUACATE**

KIWI • **EL KIWI**

MELON • **EL MELÓN**

PINEAPPLE • **LA PIÑA**

COCONUT • **EL COCO**

WATERMELON • **LA SANDÍA**

WALNUTS • **LAS NUECES**

STRAWBERRIES • **LA FRESA**

GRAPES • **LAS UVAS**

RAISINS • **LAS PASAS**

En el cuarto de estar

CEILING **EL TECHO**

CORNER **LA ESQUINA**

DOOR **LA PUERTA**

PAINTINGS **LOS CUADROS**

PORTRAIT **EL RETRATO**

LANDSCAPE **EL PAISAJE**

BLINDS **LA PERSIANA**

TELEVISION **EL TELEVISOR**

CUSHION **EL COJÍN**

IRONING BOARD **LA TABLA DE PLANCHAR**

BROOM **EL CEPILLO**

VACUUM **LA ASPIRADORA**

LAUNDRY BASKET **LA CESTA**

VASE **EL JARRÓN**

FRAME **EL MARCO**

CLOTH **EL TRAPO**

LAMP **LA LÁMPARA**

CANDLEHOLDER **EL CANDELABRO**

12

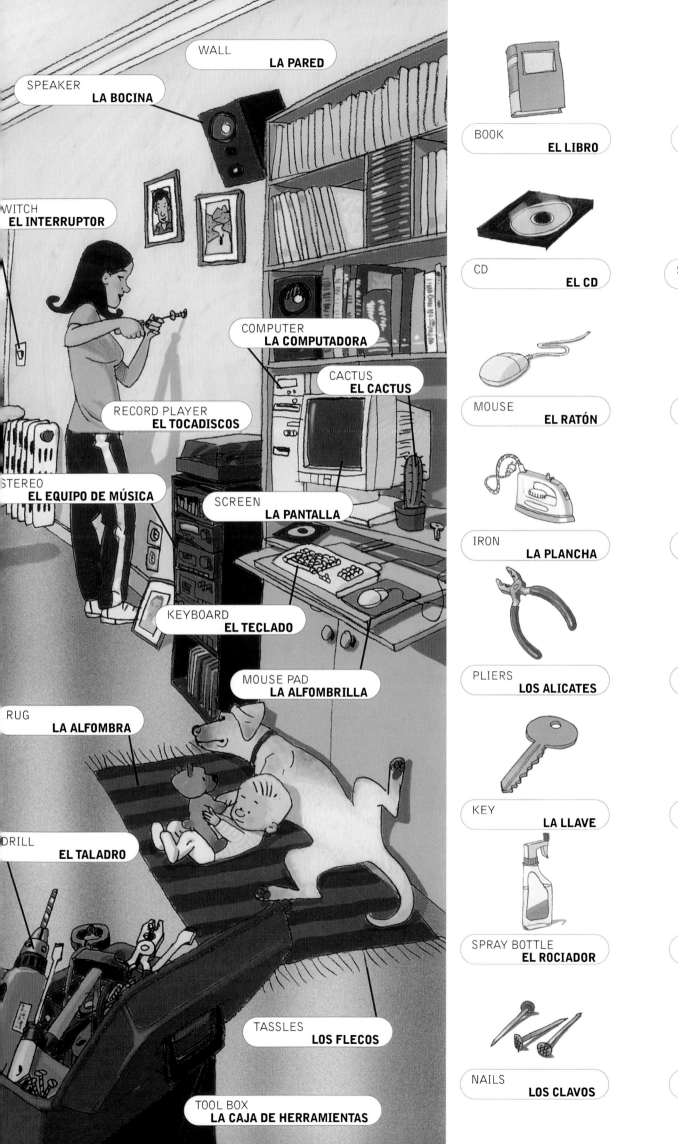

WALL
LA PARED

SPEAKER
LA BOCINA

WITCH
EL INTERRUPTOR

COMPUTER
LA COMPUTADORA

CACTUS
EL CACTUS

RECORD PLAYER
EL TOCADISCOS

STEREO
EL EQUIPO DE MÚSICA

SCREEN
LA PANTALLA

KEYBOARD
EL TECLADO

MOUSE PAD
LA ALFOMBRILLA

RUG
LA ALFOMBRA

DRILL
EL TALADRO

TASSLES
LOS FLECOS

TOOL BOX
LA CAJA DE HERRAMIENTAS

BOOK
EL LIBRO

CD
EL CD

MOUSE
EL RATÓN

IRON
LA PLANCHA

PLIERS
LOS ALICATES

KEY
LA LLAVE

SPRAY BOTTLE
EL ROCIADOR

NAILS
LOS CLAVOS

VIDEO RECORDER
EL VÍDEO

SOCKET
EL ENCHUFE

DUSTPAN
EL RECOGEDOR

FEATHER DUSTER
EL PLUMERO

HAMMER
EL MARTILLO

PINCERS
LAS TENAZAS

KEY RING
EL LLAVERO

SCREWDRIVER
EL DESTORNILLADOR

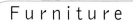

CHAIR • **LA SILLA**   ARMCHAIR • **LA BUTACA**   ROCKING CHAIR • **LA MECEDORA**   ARMCHAIR • **EL SILLÓN**

SOFA • **EL SOFÁ**   DIVAN • **EL DIVÁN**   OTTOMAN • **EL BANQUILLO**

DINING TABLE • **LA MESA DE COMEDOR**   ROUND TABLE • **LA MESA CAMILLA**   DESK • **LA MESA DE DESPACHO**

HUTCH • **LA ALACENA**

DISPLAY CABINET •
LA VITRINA

SIDEBOARD• **EL APARADOR**

BED • **LA CAMA**

CRIB • **LA CUNA**

BOOKCASE • **EL LIBRERO**

ARMOIRE • **EL ARMARIO**

DRESSER • **LA CÓMODA**

DESK • **EL ESCRITORIO**

DRESSING TABLE •
EL TOCADOR

MIRROR
EL ESPEJO

DEODORANT
EL DESODORANTE

SINK
EL LAVABO

TOWEL
LA TOALLA

KNOB
EL TIRADOR

FAUCET
EL GRIFO

PLUG
EL TAPÓN

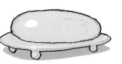

SOAP
EL JABÓN

SPONGE
LA ESPONJA

LIPSTICK
EL PINTALABIOS

COTTON SWABS
LOS BASTONICILLOS

HAIR DRYER
EL SECADOR

TALCUM POWDER
EL POLVO DE TALCO

TOOTHPASTE
LA PASTA DE DIENTES

TOOTHBRUSH
EL CEPILLO DE DIENTES

RAZOR
EL RASTRILLO

NAILBRUSH
EL CEPILLO DE UÑAS

COMB
EL PEINE

HAIRBRUSH
EL CEPILLO

POTTY
EL ORINAL

TISSUES
LOS PAÑUELOS DE PAPEL

ARM
EL BRAZO

BELLY BUTTON
EL OMBLIGO

BREAST/CHEST
EL PECHO

LEG
LA PIERNA

HAND
LA MANO

ANKLE
EL TOBILLO

FOOT
EL PIE

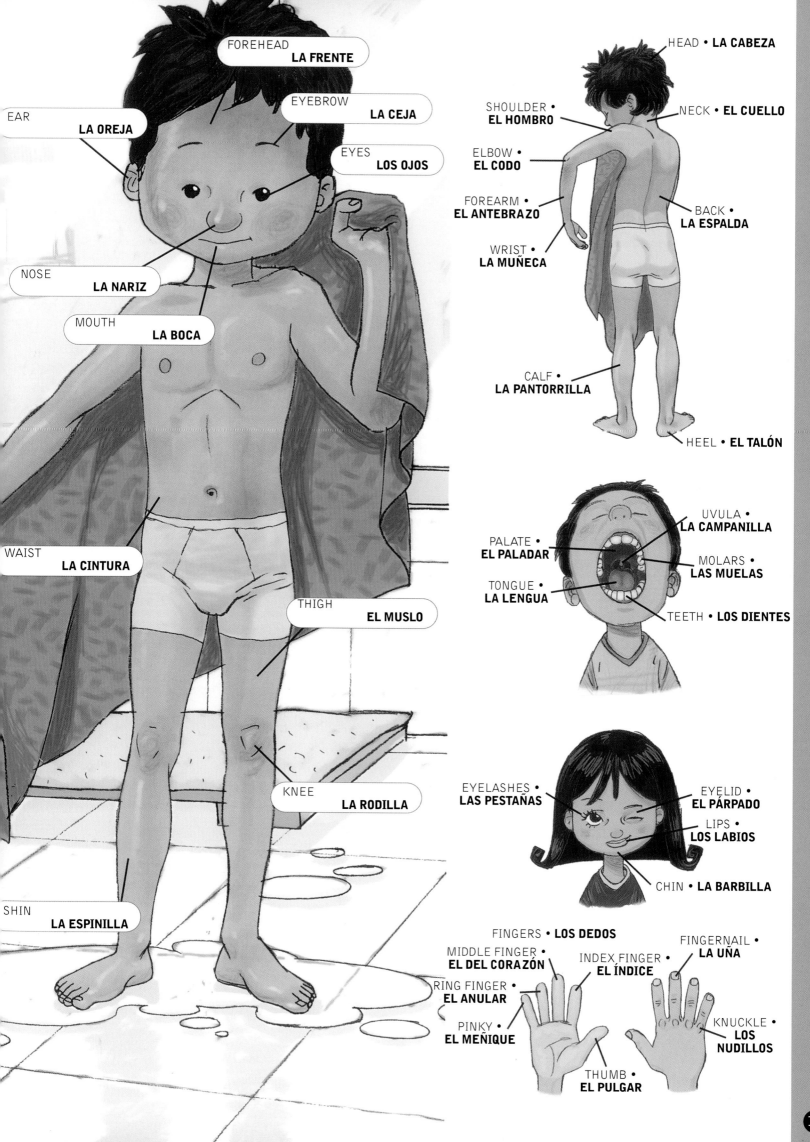

FOREHEAD **LA FRENTE**

EYEBROW **LA CEJA**

EYES **LOS OJOS**

EAR **LA OREJA**

NOSE **LA NARIZ**

MOUTH **LA BOCA**

WAIST **LA CINTURA**

THIGH **EL MUSLO**

KNEE **LA RODILLA**

SHIN **LA ESPINILLA**

HEAD • **LA CABEZA**

SHOULDER • **EL HOMBRO**

NECK • **EL CUELLO**

ELBOW • **EL CODO**

FOREARM • **EL ANTEBRAZO**

BACK **LA ESPALDA**

WRIST • **LA MUÑECA**

CALF • **LA PANTORRILLA**

HEEL • **EL TALÓN**

PALATE • **EL PALADAR**

UVULA • **LA CAMPANILLA**

TONGUE • **LA LENGUA**

MOLARS • **LAS MUELAS**

TEETH • **LOS DIENTES**

EYELASHES • **LAS PESTAÑAS**

EYELID • **EL PÁRPADO**

LIPS • **LOS LABIOS**

CHIN • **LA BARBILLA**

FINGERS • **LOS DEDOS**

MIDDLE FINGER • **EL DEL CORAZÓN**

INDEX FINGER • **EL ÍNDICE**

FINGERNAIL • **LA UÑA**

RING FINGER • **EL ANULAR**

PINKY • **EL MEÑIQUE**

KNUCKLE **LOS NUDILLOS**

THUMB • **EL PULGAR**

In the bedroom
En el dormitorio

ROBOT **EL ROBOT**

READING LAMP **EL FLEXO**

BEDSPREAD **LA COLCHA**

RACKET **LA RAQUETA**

LADDER **LA ESCALERA**

POSTER **EL PÓSTER**

TRUNK **EL BAÚL**

PILLOW **LA ALMOHADA**

COMFORTER **EL EDREDÓN**

CRIB **LA CUNA**

PAJAMAS **EL PIJAMA**

DIAPER **EL PAÑAL**

BLANKET **LA MANTA**

SHEET **LA SÁBANA**

MATTRESS **EL COLCHÓN**

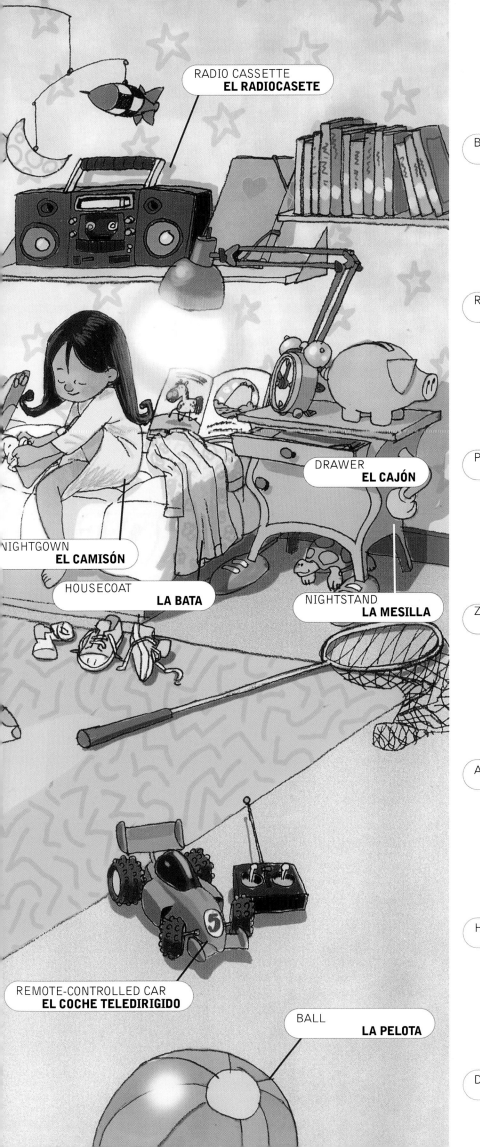

RADIO CASSETTE
EL RADIOCASETE

DRAWER
EL CAJÓN

NIGHTGOWN
EL CAMISÓN

HOUSECOAT
LA BATA

NIGHTSTAND
LA MESILLA

REMOTE-CONTROLLED CAR
EL COCHE TELEDIRIGIDO

BALL
LA PELOTA

BOTTLE
EL BIBERÓN

PACIFIER
EL CHUPETE

RATTLE
EL SONAJERO

BUTTON
EL BOTÓN

PIGGY BANK
LA ALCANCÍA

BUTTONHOLE
EL OJAL

ZIPPER
LA CREMALLERA

LACES
LOS CORDONES

ALARM CLOCK
EL DESPERTADOR

STORYBOOK
EL CUENTO

HANGER
EL GANCHO

FOLDER
LA CARPETA

DINOSAUR
EL DINOSAURIO

DOLL
EL MUÑECO

PANTIES •
LAS PANTALETAS

UNDERPANTS •
LOS CALZONCILLOS

SOCKS • **LOS CALCETINES**

TIGHTS • **LOS LEOTARDOS**

T-SHIRT • **LA CAMISETA**

KNITTED SHIRT • **EL POLO**

SHIRT • **LA CAMISA**

CARDIGAN • **LA CHAQUETA**

SWEATER • **EL JERSEY**

VEST• **EL CHALECO**

DRESS • **EL VESTIDO**

JUMPER • **EL PICHI**

SKIRT • **LA FALDA**

SHORTS • **EL PANTALÓN CORTO**

PANTS • **EL PANTALÓN LARGO**

OVERALLS •
EL PANTALÓN DE PETO

COAT • **EL ABRIGO**

JEAN JACKET • **LA CHAQUETA**

RAINCOAT •
EL IMPERMEABLE

SHOES • **LOS ZAPATOS**

SNEAKERS • **LAS ZAPATILLAS**

SANDALS • **LAS SANDALIAS**

BOOTS • **LAS BOTAS**

HAT • **EL GORRO**

SWIMMING TRUNKS •
EL TRAJE DE BAÑO DE NIÑO

SWIMSUIT •
EL TRAJE DE BAÑO DE NIÑA

TO KISS **BESAR**

TO HUG **ABRAZAR**

TO PET **ACARICIAR**

TO LOOK AT **VER**

TO LISTEN **OÍR**

TO TASTE **GUSTAR**

TO SMELL **OLER**

TO TOUCH **TOCAR**

TO EAT **COMER**

TO DRINK **BEBER**

TO SERVE **SERVIR**

TO COOK **COCINAR**

TO SPREAD **UNTAR**

TO BREAK **PARTIR**

TO PEEL **PELAR**

TO WHISK **BATIR**

TO DO THE WASHING-UP **LAVAR LOS PLATOS**

TO BLOW **SOPLAR**

TO GIVE A PRESENT **REGALAR**

TO CLEAN **LIMPIAR**

TO SWEEP **BARRER**

TO MOP **FREGAR**

TO IRON **PLANCHAR**

TO HANG UP **TENDER**

TO TAKE A BATH **BAÑARSE**

TO DRY ONESELF **SECARSE**

TO BRUSH **CEPILLAR**

TO GET DIRTY **MANCHARSE**

TO WASH ONESELF **LAVARSE**

TO SHAVE **AFEITARSE**

TO CUT ONE'S NAILS **CORTARSE LAS UÑAS**

TO GO TO BED **ACOSTARSE**

TO GET UP **LEVANTARSE**

TO SLEEP **DORMIR**

TO MAKE ONE'S BED **HACER LA CAMA**

TO STRETCH **ESTIRARSE**

TO YAWN **BOSTEZAR**

TO COMB ONE'S HAIR **PEINARSE**

TO GET DRESSED **VESTIRSE**

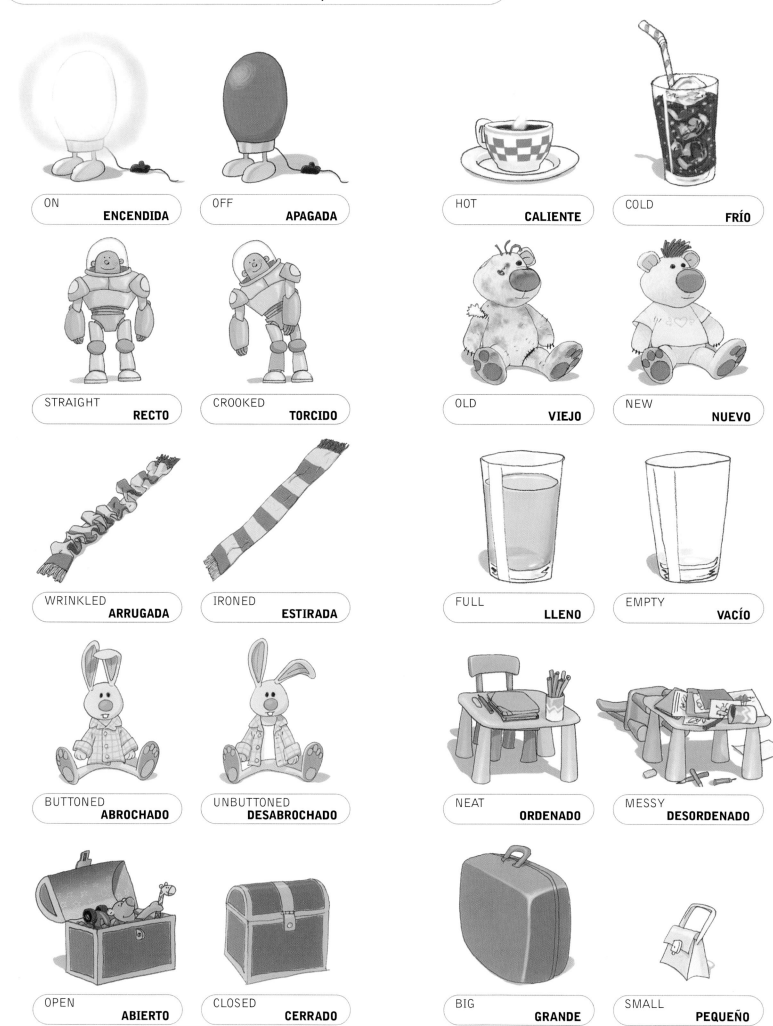

ON **ENCENDIDA**

OFF **APAGADA**

HOT **CALIENTE**

COLD **FRÍO**

STRAIGHT **RECTO**

CROOKED **TORCIDO**

OLD **VIEJO**

NEW **NUEVO**

WRINKLED **ARRUGADA**

IRONED **ESTIRADA**

FULL **LLENO**

EMPTY **VACÍO**

BUTTONED **ABROCHADO**

UNBUTTONED **DESABROCHADO**

NEAT **ORDENADO**

MESSY **DESORDENADO**

OPEN **ABIERTO**

CLOSED **CERRADO**

BIG **GRANDE**

SMALL **PEQUEÑO**

DIRTY **SUCIA**

CLEAN **LIMPIA**

COMBED **PEINADO**

UNCOMBED **DESPEINADO**

BAREFOOT **DESCALZO**

WITH SHOES ON **CALZADO**

COMFORTABLE **CÓMODA**

UNCOMFORTABLE **INCÓMODA**

ASLEEP **DORMIDO**

AWAKE **DESPIERTO**

UNDRESSED **DESVESTIDO**

DRESSED **VESTIDO**

DRY **SECA**

WET **MOJADA**

HAPPY **CONTENTO**

SAD **TRISTE**

En clase

LETTERS
LAS LETRAS

PIECES OF CHALK
LAS TIZAS

STUDENTS
LOS ALUMNOS

SHOOTS
LOS BROTES

PHOTOGRAPH
LA FOTOGRAFÍA

BACKPACK
LA MOCHILA

TEACHER
LA PROFESORA

CLOTHES RACK
EL PERCHERO

SHEET OF PAPER
LA HOJA

WATERCOLORS
LAS ACUARELAS

PAINTS
LAS PINTURAS

CASE
EL ESTUCHE

BLACKBOARD
LA PIZARRA

DRAWINGS
LOS DIBUJOS

EASEL
EL CABALLETE

GIRL
LA NIÑA

ASTEPAPER BIN
LA PAPELERA

BOY
EL NIÑO

JARS
LOS BOTES

CLAY
LA PLASTILINA

MAP
EL MAPA

SCISSORS
LAS TIJERAS

ERASER
EL BORRADOR

PENCIL
EL LÁPIZ

PENCIL SHARPENER
EL SACAPUNTAS

ERASER
LA GOMA

PEN
EL BOLÍGRAFO

MARKER
EL ROTULADOR

GLUE
LA PEGA

TAPE
EL PAPEL CELO

BALL
EL OVILLO

PAINTBRUSH
EL PINCEL

BINDER
EL ÁLBUM

RULER
LA REGLA

Colors
Los colores

MAROON
EL GRANATE

LIGHT BLUE
EL AZUL CLARO

LIGHT GREEN
EL VERDE CLARO

PURPLE
EL MORADO

BROWN
EL MARRÓN

RED
EL ROJO

GRAY
EL GRIS

ORANGE
EL NARANJA

DARK GREEN
EL VERDE OSCURO

YELLOW
EL AMARILLO

BLACK
EL NEGRO

WHITE
EL BLANCO

PINK
EL ROSA

OCHRE
EL OCRE

DARK BLUE
EL AZUL OSCURO

Shapes
Las formas

TRIANGLE
EL TRIÁNGULO

CIRCLE
EL CÍRCULO

HALF MOON
LA MEDIALUNA

SQUARE
EL CUADRADO

RECTANGLE
EL RECTÁNGULO

STAR
LA ESTRELLA

HEART
EL CORAZÓN

OVAL
EL ÓVALO

a b c d e f

g h i j k l

m n ñ o p

q r s t u

v w x y z

Time
El tiempo

MONDAY
EL LUNES

TUESDAY
EL MARTES

WEDNESDAY
EL MIÉRCOLES

THURSDAY
EL JUEVES

FRIDAY
EL VIERNES

SATURDAY
EL SÁBADO

SUNDAY
EL DOMINGO

THE SEASONS
LAS ESTACIONES

SPRING
LA PRIMAVERA

SUMMER
EL VERANO

AUTUMN/FALL
EL OTOÑO

WINTER
EL INVIERNO

THE MONTHS OF THE YEAR
LOS MESES DEL AÑO

JANUARY
ENERO

FEBRUARY
FEBRERO

MARCH
MARZO

APRIL
ABRIL

MAY
MAYO

JUNE
JUNIO

JULY
JULIO

AUGUST
AGOSTO

SEPTEMBER
SEPTIEMBRE

OCTOBER
OCTUBRE

NOVEMBER
NOVIEMBRE

DECEMBER
DICIEMBRE

Numbers
Los números

ONE **UNO**

TWO **DOS**

THREE **TRES**

FOUR **CUATRO**

FIVE **CINCO**

SIX **SIES**

SEVEN **SIETE**

EIGHT **OCHO**

NINE **NUEVE**

TEN **DIEZ**

FIRST **PRIMERA** SECOND **SEGUNDA** THIRD **TERCERO** FOURTH **CUARTO** FIFTH **QUINTA** SIXTH **SEXTA** SEVENTH **SÉPTIMO** EIGHTH **OCTAVA** NINTH **NOVENO** TENTH **DÉCIMO**

At recess
En el recreo

PIPE **LA CAÑERÍA**

BASKET **LA CANASTA**

HIDE-AND-SEEK **EL ESCONDIT**

RAILINGS **LA VERJA**

GARDENER **EL JARDINERO**

LINE **LA FILA**

WATER **EL AGUA**

HOSE **LA MANGUERA**

WATER FOUNTAIN **LA FUENTE**

WHEELCHAIR **LA SILLA DE RUEDAS**

PONYTAIL **LA COLETA**

JUMP ROPE **LA COMBA**

GOAL **LA PORTERÍA**

BALL **EL BALÓN**

GOALIE **EL PORTERO**

MARBLES **LAS CANICAS**

CARDS **LAS CARTAS**

BANISTER **LA BARANDILLA**

RAMP **LA RAMPA**

CIRCLE **EL CÍRCULO**

BRAIDS **LAS TRENZAS**

PICTURES **LAS FOTOS**

ALBUM **EL ÁLBUM**

WHISTLE **EL SILBATO**

TOP **EL TROMPO**

YO-YO **EL YOYÓ**

MEDAL **LA MEDALLA**

FLOWERPOT **LA MACETA**

WINDOW BOX **LA JARDINERA**

COMIC **LA TIRA CÓMICA**

GLASSES **LAS GAFAS**

COOKIES **LAS GALLETAS**

CRUTCH **LA MULETA**

RIBBON **EL LAZO**

HEADBAND **LA DIADEMA**

BARRETTE **LA HORQUILLA**

BRACELET **LA PULSERA**

NECKLACE **EL COLLAR**

RING **LA SORTIJA**

35

ROPE
LA CUERDA DE NUDOS

WALL BARS
LAS ESPALDERAS

WINDOW LADDER
LA ESCALA

CRAWLING TUNNEL
EL TÚNEL DE GATEO

PIKE
LA PICA

LEOTARD
LA MALLA

TRACKSUIT
EL CHÁNDAL

KNEE PAD
LA RODILLERA

MAT
LA COLCHONETA

SWEAT
EL SUD

RIBBON
LA CINTA

SNEAKERS
LOS ZAPATOS DE TENIS

CLUB
LA MAZA

RINGS
LAS ANILLAS

TRAMPOLINE
LA CAMA ELÁSTICA

SPRINGBOARD
EL TRAMPOLÍN

HOOP
EL ARO

CUBE
EL CUBO

SOMERSAULT
LA VOLTERETA

WATCH
EL RELOJ DE PULSERA

STOPWATCH
EL CRONÓMETRO

VAULTING BOX
EL PLINTO

VAULTING HORSE
EL POTRO

PARALLEL BARS
LAS PARALELAS

FIRE EXTINGUISHER
EL EXTINTOR

FLUORESCENT LIGHT
EL FLUORESCENTE

Sports

Deportes

GOLF • **EL GOLF**   TENNIS • **EL TENIS**   HORSEBACK RIDING • **LA HÍPICA**

BASEBALL • **EL BÉISBOL**   HOCKEY • **EL HOCKEY**   RUGBY • **EL RUGBY**

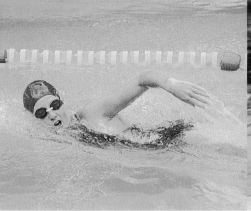

SKIING • **EL ESQUÍ**   SWIMMING • **LA NATACIÓN**   CYCLING • **EL CICLISMO**   SKATING • **EL PATINAJE**

SOCCER • **EL FÚTBOL**   BASKETBALL • **EL BALONCESTO**   HANDBALL • **EL BALONMANO**   VOLLEYBALL • **EL VOLEIBOL**

PING-PONG • **EL PING-PONG**   MARTIAL ARTS • **LAS ARTES MARCIALES**   RACE • **LA CARRERA**

HIGH JUMP •
EL SALTO DE ALTURA   HURDLE JUMP •
EL SALTO DE VALLAS   LONG JUMP •
EL SALTO DE LONGITUD   FENCING • **LA ESGRIMA**

HIKING •
EL MONTAÑISMO   CLIMBING •
LA ESCALADA   CANOEING • **EL PIRAGÜISMO**   HANG GLIDING • **EL ALA DELTA**

NOWBOARDING • **EL SNOWBOARD**   WINDSURFING •
EL WINDSURF   BUNGEE JUMPING • **EL PUENTING**   RAFTING • **EL RAFTING**

SPOTLIGHTS **LOS FOCOS**

FAIRY **EL HADA**

MOON **LA LUNA**

MOUSTACHE **EL BIGOTE**

MONSTER **EL MONSTRUO**

EXIT **LA SALIDA**

GOATEE **LA PERILLA**

MUSHROOM **LA SETA**

BEARD **LA BARBA**

GHOST **EL FANTASMA**

WALKING STICK **EL BASTÓN**

USHER **LA ACOMODADORA**

HANDBELL **LA CAMPANILLA**

DRAGON **EL DRAGO**

TREASURE **EL TESORO**

STAGE **EL ESCENARIO**

SPECTATORS **LOS ESPECTADORES**

SEATS **LAS BUTACAS**

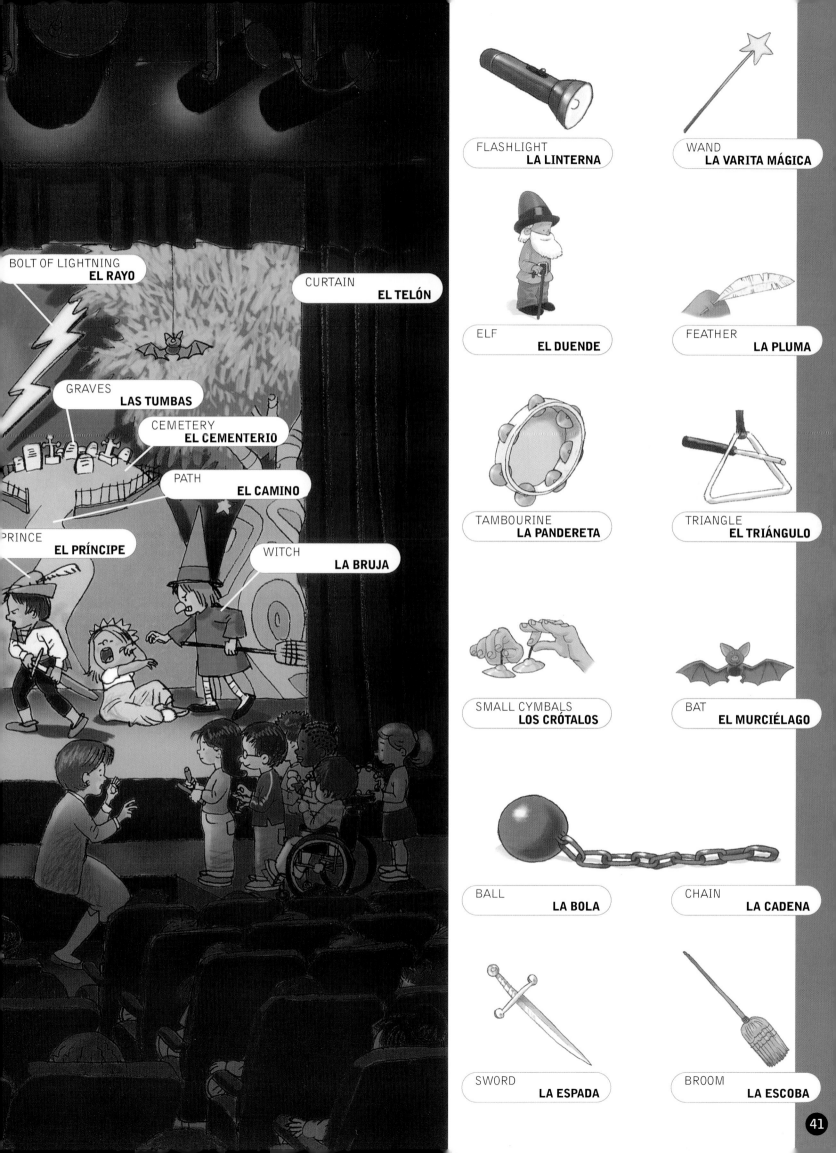

BOLT OF LIGHTNING **EL RAYO**

CURTAIN **EL TELÓN**

GRAVES **LAS TUMBAS**

CEMETERY **EL CEMENTERIO**

PATH **EL CAMINO**

PRINCE **EL PRÍNCIPE**

WITCH **LA BRUJA**

FLASHLIGHT **LA LINTERNA**

WAND **LA VARITA MÁGICA**

ELF **EL DUENDE**

FEATHER **LA PLUMA**

TAMBOURINE **LA PANDERETA**

TRIANGLE **EL TRIÁNGULO**

SMALL CYMBALS **LOS CRÓTALOS**

BAT **EL MURCIÉLAGO**

BALL **LA BOLA**

CHAIN **LA CADENA**

SWORD **LA ESPADA**

BROOM **LA ESCOBA**

STRING INSTRUMENTS • INSTRUMENTOS DE CUERDA

GUITAR • **LA GUITARRA**

ELECTRIC GUITAR •
LA GUITARRA ELÉCTRICA

BANJO • **EL BANJO**

VIOLIN • **EL VIOLÍN**

VIOLA • **LA VIOLA**

CELLO • **EL VIOLONCHELO**

DOUBLE BASS •
EL CONTRABAJO

PERCUSSION INSTRUMENTS • INSTRUMENTOS DE PERCUSIÓN

MARACAS • **LAS MARACAS**

CASTANETS • **LAS CASTAÑUELAS**

TAMBOURINE • **LA PANDERETA**

DRUM • **EL TAMBOR**

CHINESE BOX • **LA CAJA CHINA**

XYLOPHONE • **EL XILOFÓN**

CONGA DRUMS • **LAS CONGAS**

KETTLE DRUM • **EL TIMBAL**

DRUM SET • **LA BATERÍA**

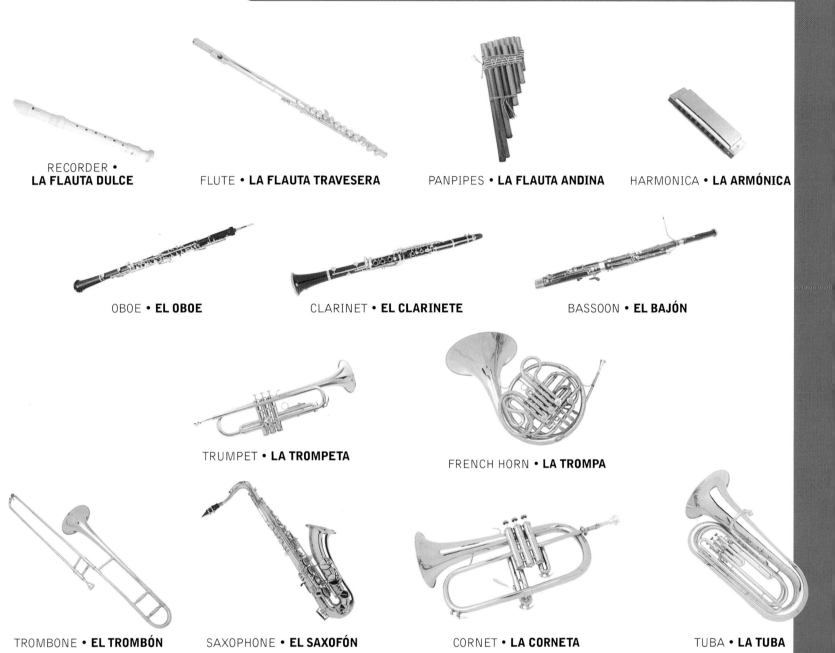

RECORDER •
LA FLAUTA DULCE

FLUTE • **LA FLAUTA TRAVESERA**

PANPIPES • **LA FLAUTA ANDINA**

HARMONICA • **LA ARMÓNICA**

OBOE • **EL OBOE**

CLARINET • **EL CLARINETE**

BASSOON • **EL BAJÓN**

TRUMPET • **LA TROMPETA**

FRENCH HORN • **LA TROMPA**

TROMBONE • **EL TROMBÓN**

SAXOPHONE • **EL SAXOFÓN**

CORNET • **LA CORNETA**

TUBA • **LA TUBA**

KEYBOARD INSTRUMENTS • **INSTRUMENTOS CON TECLADO**

ACCORDION • **EL ACORDEÓN**

ORGAN • **EL ÓRGANO**

PIANO • **EL PIANO**

WINDMILL **EL MOLINO**

BARN **EL ESTABLO**

STABLE **LA CUADRA**

HORSE **EL CABALLO**

BEAM **LA VIGA**

MARE **LA YEGUA**

PIGSTY **LA POCILGA**

MANE **LOS CRINES**

DUCK **EL PATO**

PONY **EL POTRO**

FARMER **EL GRANJERO**

TROUGH **EL PESEBRE**

BUNNY **EL GAZA**

RABBIT **EL CONEJO**

PEN **EL REDIL**

HENS **LAS GALLINAS**

RAM **EL CARNERO**

CHICKS **LOS POLLOS**

GOAT **LA CABRA**

HAYLOFT **EL PAJAR**

CHIMNEY **LA CHIMENEA**

POND **LA CHARCA**

BULL **EL TORO**

CALF **EL TERNERO**

COW **LA VACA**

REINS **LAS RIENDAS**

SADDLE **LA SILLA DE MONTAR**

DONKEY **EL BURRO**

PUPPY **EL CACHORRO**

GOOSE **LA OCA**

TOAD **EL SAPO**

TURKEY **EL PAVO**

ROOSTER **EL GALLO**

SHEEP **LA OVEJA**

DOG **EL PERRO**

PIGLET **EL LECHÓN**

PIG **EL CERDO**

HOE **LA AZADA**

RAKE **EL RASTRILLO**

FIREWOOD **LA LEÑA**

AXE **EL HACHA**

BELL **EL CENCERRO**

SADDLEBAG **LAS ALFORJAS**

BARREL **EL BARRIL**

WEATHER VANE **LA VELETA**

45

Los animales

LION • **EL LEÓN**   TIGER • **EL TIGRE**   PANTHER • **LA PANTERA**

LEOPARD • **EL LEOPARDO**   PUMA • **EL PUMA**   LYNX • **EL LINCE**

ELEPHANT • **EL ELEFANTE**   HIPPOPOTAMUS • **EL HIPOPÓTAMO**   RHINO • **EL RINOCERONTE**

LLAMA • **LA LLAMA**   GIRAFFE • **LA JIRAFA**   ZEBRA • **LA CEBRA**

BROWN BEAR • **EL OSO PARDO** POLAR BEAR • **EL OSO POLAR** PANDA BEAR • **EL OSO PANDA**

CHIMPANZEE • **EL CHIMPANCÉ** GORILLA • **EL GORILA** ORANGUTAN • **EL ORANGUTÁN**

DROMEDARY • **EL DROMEDARIO** CAMEL • **EL CAMELLO** KOALA • **EL KOALA**

TORTOISE • **LA TORTUGA** SNAKE • **LA SERPIENTE** KANGAROO • **EL CANGURO**

TO READ **LEER**

TO SPEAK **HABLAR**

TO LISTEN **ESCUCHAR**

TO WRITE **ESCRIBIR**

TO COUNT **CONTAR**

TO PLAY **JUGAR**

TO GLUE **PEGAR**

TO DRAW **DIBUJAR**

TO COLOR **COLOREAR**

TO SHAPE **MODELAR**

TO ERASE **BORRAR**

TO CROSS OUT **TACHAR**

TO CUT **CORTAR**

TO SHARPEN **SACAR PUNTA**

TO EXPLAIN **EXPLICAR**

TO PLAY AN INSTRUMENT **TOCAR UN INSTRUMENTO**

TO JOIN **UNIR**

TO SEPARATE **SEPARAR**

TO WRAP **ENVOLVER**

TO UNWRAP **DESENVOLVER**

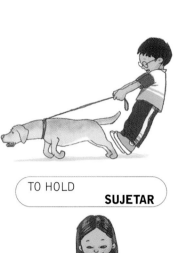

TO HOLD **SUJETAR**

TO LET GO OF **SOLTAR**

TO TIE UP **ATAR**

TO UNTIE **DESATAR**

TO BOUNCE **BOTAR**

TO JUMP **SALTAR**

TO HIDE **ESCONDERSE**

TO THROW **TIRAR**

TO TURN SOMERSAULTS **DAR UNA VOLTERETA**

TO KICK **DAR UNA PATADA**

TO SWEAT **SUDAR**

TO LIGHT **ALUMBRAR**

TO BUTTON **ABROCHAR**

TO UNBUTTON **DESABROCHAR**

TO PUSH **EMPUJAR**

TO DRAG **ARRASTRAR**

TO SEW **COSER**

TO MAKE UP **MAQUILLAR**

TO PERFORM **ACTUAR**

TO GREET **SALUDAR**

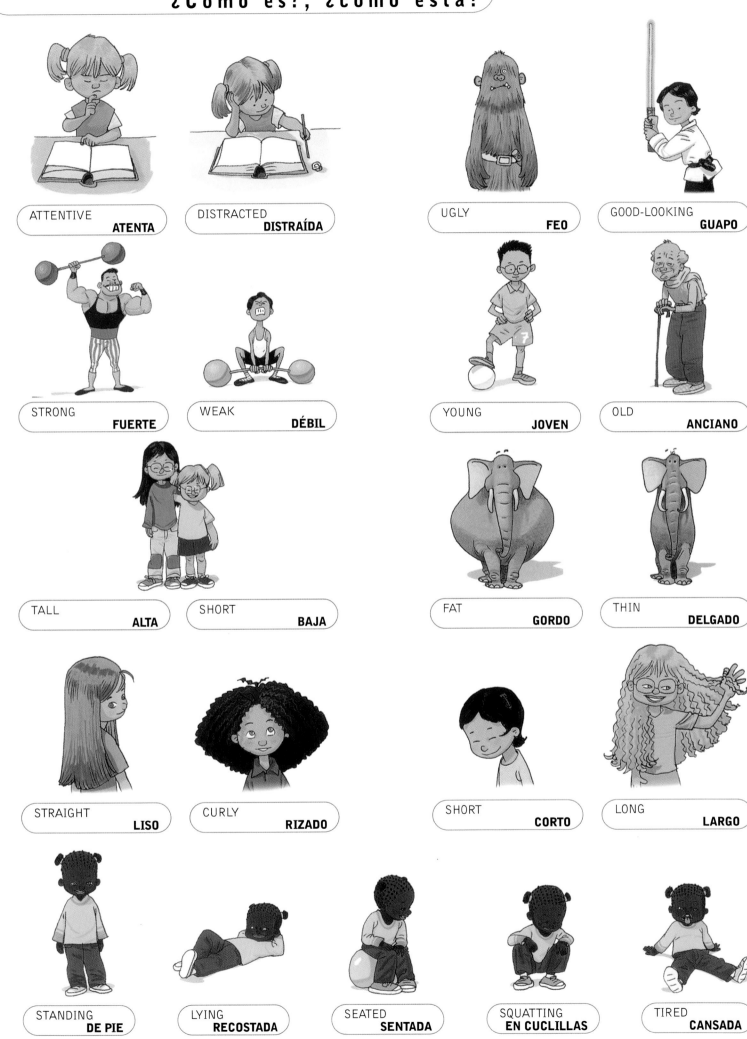

ATTENTIVE **ATENTA**

DISTRACTED **DISTRAÍDA**

UGLY **FEO**

GOOD-LOOKING **GUAPO**

STRONG **FUERTE**

WEAK **DÉBIL**

YOUNG **JOVEN**

OLD **ANCIANO**

TALL **ALTA**

SHORT **BAJA**

FAT **GORDO**

THIN **DELGADO**

STRAIGHT **LISO**

CURLY **RIZADO**

SHORT **CORTO**

LONG **LARGO**

STANDING **DE PIE**

LYING **RECOSTADA**

SEATED **SENTADA**

SQUATTING **EN CUCLILLAS**

TIRED **CANSADA**

Where are they?

¿Dónde está?

UP **ARRIBA**

DOWN **ABAJO**

IN FRONT OF **DELANTE**

BEHIND **DETRÁS**

ON **ENCIMA**

UNDER **DEBAJO**

IN **DENTRO**

OUT **FUERA**

FAR **LEJOS**

NEAR **CERCA**

NEXT TO **AL LADO DE**

AROUND **ALREDEDOR**

THROUGH **A TRAVÉS DE**

BETWEEN **ENTRE**

OPPOSITE **ENFRENTE**

FROM **DESDE**

TOWARD **HACIA**

TO **HASTA**

51

Walking around

De paseo

BALCONIES **LOS BALCONES**

MOVIE THEATER **EL CINE**

CHURCH **LA IGLESIA**

HOTEL **EL HOTEL**

POST OFFICE **EL CORREO**

STORE **LA TIENDA**

BREAKDOWN **LA AVERÍA**

DRAIN **LA ALCANTARILLA**

SLIDE **LA CHORRERA**

BENCH **EL BANCO**

PARK **EL PARQUE**

BUS STOP **LA PARADA DE AUTOBÚS**

MEMORIAL **EL MONUMENTO**

PIGEONS **LAS PALOMAS**

CRUMBS **LAS MIGAS**

PUDDLE **EL CHARCO**

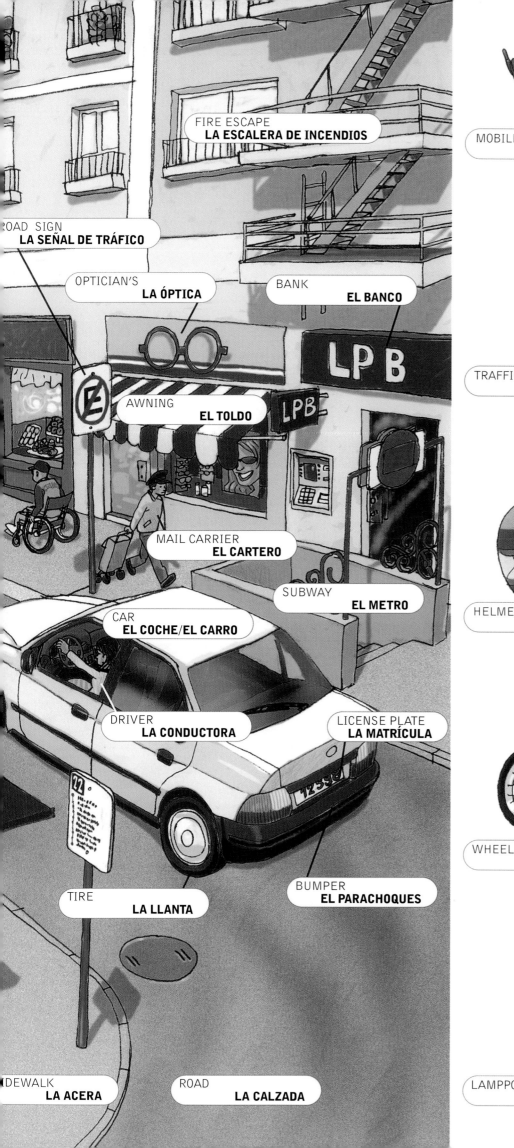

FIRE ESCAPE **LA ESCALERA DE INCENDIOS**

ROAD SIGN **LA SEÑAL DE TRÁFICO**

OPTICIAN'S **LA ÓPTICA**

BANK **EL BANCO**

AWNING **EL TOLDO**

MAIL CARRIER **EL CARTERO**

SUBWAY **EL METRO**

CAR **EL COCHE/EL CARRO**

DRIVER **LA CONDUCTORA**

LICENSE PLATE **LA MATRÍCULA**

TIRE **LA LLANTA**

BUMPER **EL PARACHOQUES**

DEWALK **LA ACERA**

ROAD **LA CALZADA**

MOBILE PHONE **EL CELULAR**

MAILBOX **EL BUZÓN**

TRAFFIC LIGHT **EL SEMÁFORO**

CAKES **LOS PASTELES**

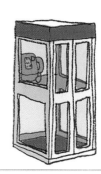

HELMET **EL CASCO**

PHONE BOOTH **LA CABINA TELEFÓNICA**

WHEEL **LA RUEDA**

FLAG **LA BANDERA**

LAMPPOST **EL FAROL**

ATM **EL CAJERO AUTOMÁTICO**

BICYCLE • **LA BICICLETA**

SKATES • **LOS PATINES**

SCOOTER • **EL PATINETE**

SKATEBOARD • **EL MONOPATÍN**

TRICYCLE • **EL TRICICLO**

WALKIE-TALKIE • **EL WALKIE-TALKIE**

LEGO BRICKS • **LAS CONSTRUCCIONES**

TEDDY BEAR • **EL OSO DE PELUCHE**

JIGSAW PUZZLE • **EL ROMPECABEZAS**

PUZZLE • **EL ROMPECABEZAS**

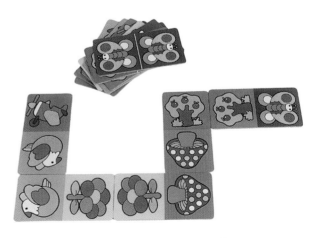

DOMINOES • **EL DOMINÓ**

ELECTRONIC GAME •
EL JUEGO ELECTRÓNICO

DOLL • **LA MUÑECA**

CAR • **EL COCHECITO**

CHESS • **EL AJEDREZ**

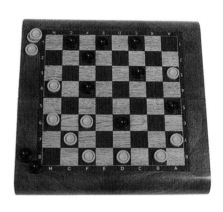

CHECKERS • **LAS DAMAS**

PARCHEESI • **EL PARCHÍS**

BOWLING • **LOS BOLOS**

PUPPETS • **LOS TÍTERES**

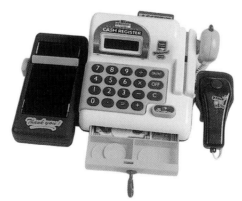

CASH REGISTER •
LA CAJA REGISTRADORA

ROCKING HORSE • **EL BALANCÍN**

En el supermercado

FRUIT STALL
LA FRUTERÍA

FISHMONGER
LA PESCADERA

BUTCHER'S
LA CARNICERÍA

BUTCHER
EL CARNICERO

APRON
EL DELANTAL

COUNTER
EL MOSTRADOR

MEAT
LA CARNE

FISH
EL PESCADO

FRUIT
LA FRUTA

CANNED FOOD
LAS CONSERVAS

BANNER
EL BANDERÍN

CASHIER
LA CAJERA

CONTAINER
EL CONTENEDOR

STROLLER
LA SILLITA

SHOPPING CART
EL CARRO

FROZEN FOOD
LOS CONGELADOS

COIN PURSE
LA CARTERITA

COINS
LAS MONEDAS

WALLET
LA BILLETERA

PURSE
EL BOLSO

MITTENS
LAS MANOPLAS

GLOVES
LOS GUANTES

HAT
EL GORRO

SCARF
EL PAÑUELO

SCARF
LA BUFANDA

BAR CODE
EL CÓDIGO DE BARRAS

BASKET
LA CESTA

SCALES
LA BALANZA

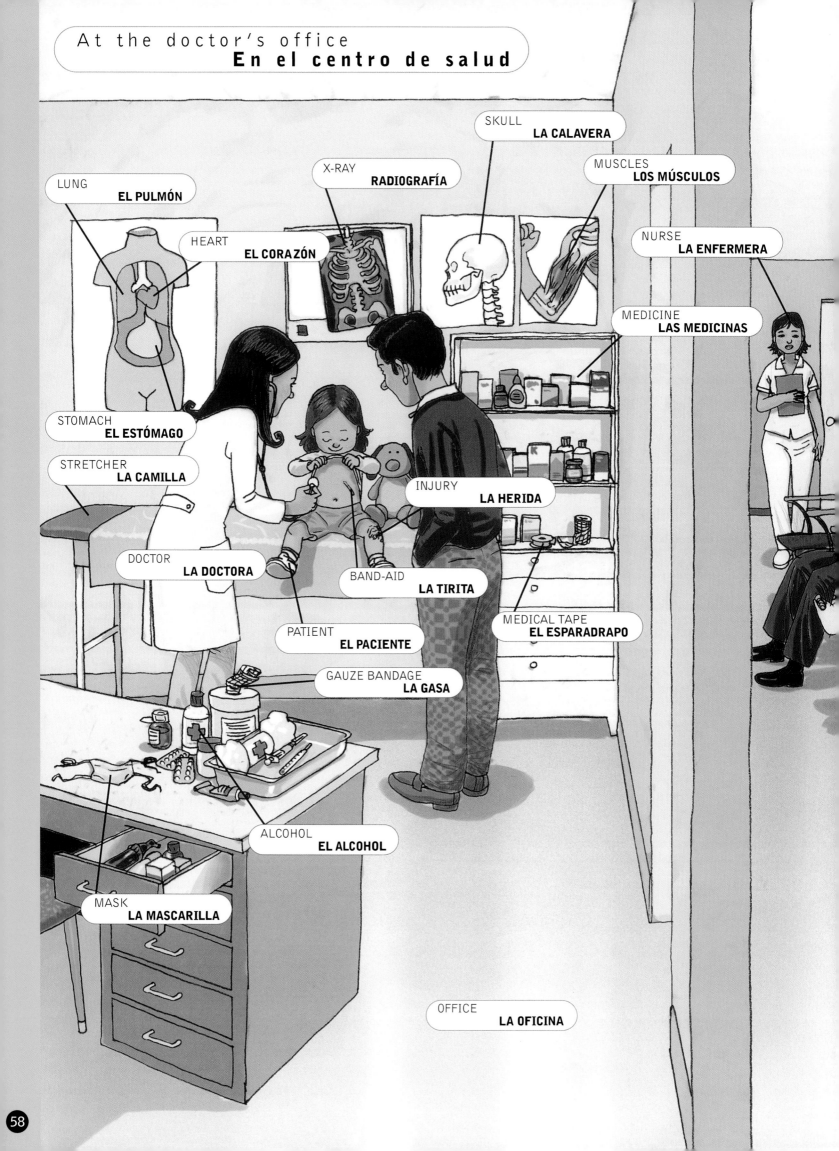

SKULL
LA CALAVERA

X-RAY
RADIOGRAFÍA

MUSCLES
LOS MÚSCULOS

LUNG
EL PULMÓN

HEART
EL CORAZÓN

NURSE
LA ENFERMERA

MEDICINE
LAS MEDICINAS

STOMACH
EL ESTÓMAGO

STRETCHER
LA CAMILLA

INJURY
LA HERIDA

DOCTOR
LA DOCTORA

BAND-AID
LA TIRITA

MEDICAL TAPE
EL ESPARADRAPO

PATIENT
EL PACIENTE

GAUZE BANDAGE
LA GASA

ALCOHOL
EL ALCOHOL

MASK
LA MASCARILLA

OFFICE
LA OFICINA

BATHROOMS
LOS SERVICIOS

SIGN
EL CARTEL

CAST
EL YESO

SEAT
EL ASIENTO

WAITING ROOM
LA SALA DE ESPERA

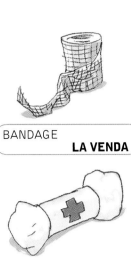

BANDAGE
LA VENDA

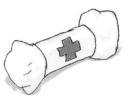

COTTON
EL ALGODÓN

SYRINGE
LA JERINGUILLA

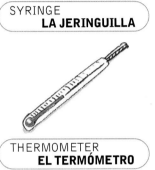

THERMOMETER
EL TERMÓMETRO

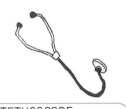

STETHOSCOPE
EL FONENDOSCOPIO

SYRUP
EL JARABE

PILLS
LAS PASTILLAS

OINTMENT
LA POMADA

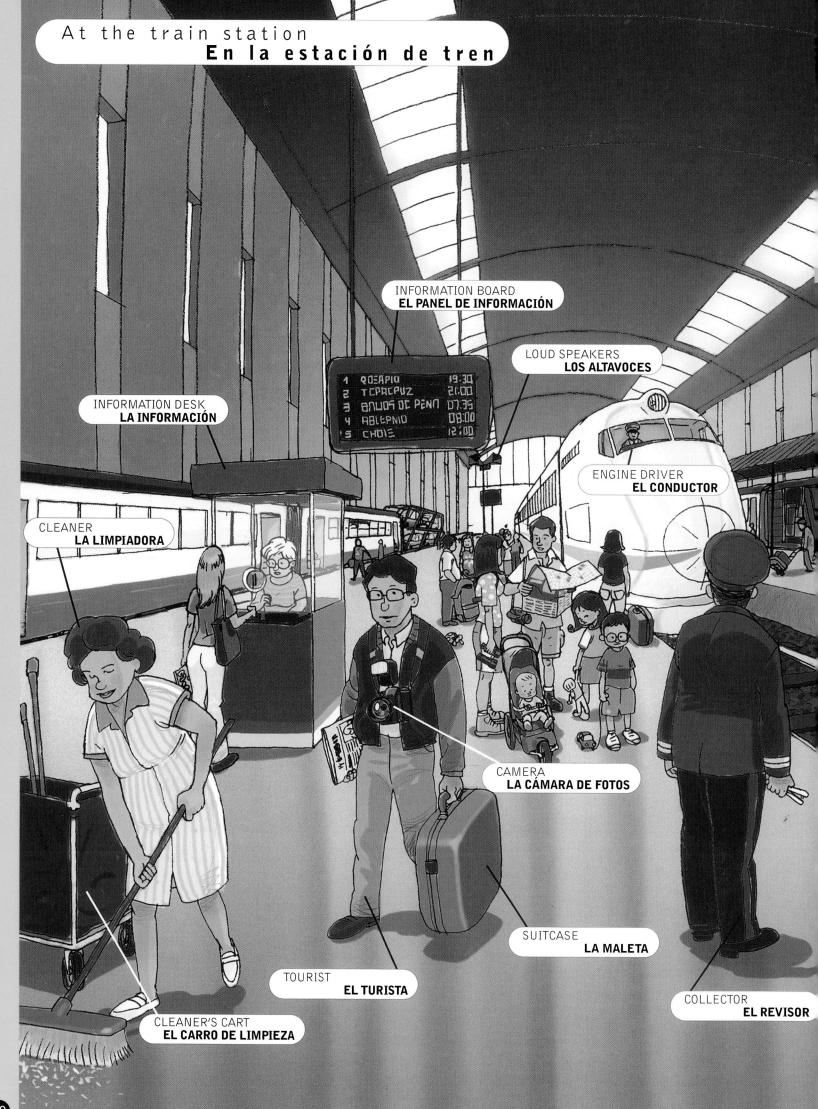

INFORMATION BOARD
EL PANEL DE INFORMACIÓN

LOUD SPEAKERS
LOS ALTAVOCES

INFORMATION DESK
LA INFORMACIÓN

ENGINE DRIVER
EL CONDUCTOR

CLEANER
LA LIMPIADORA

CAMERA
LA CÁMARA DE FOTOS

SUITCASE
LA MALETA

TOURIST
EL TURISTA

COLLECTOR
EL REVISOR

CLEANER'S CART
EL CARRO DE LIMPIEZA

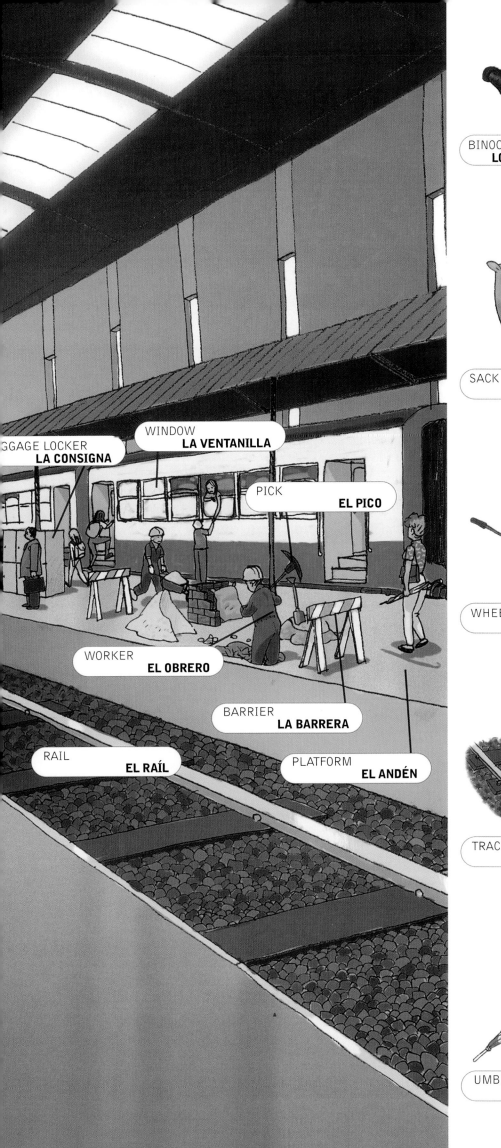

GGAGE LOCKER
LA CONSIGNA

WINDOW
LA VENTANILLA

PICK
EL PICO

WORKER
EL OBRERO

BARRIER
LA BARRERA

RAIL
EL RAÍL

PLATFORM
EL ANDÉN

BINOCULARS
LOS PRISMÁTICOS

PASSENGER CAR
EL VAGÓN DE PASAJEROS

SACK
EL SACO

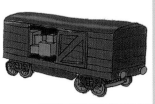

FREIGHT CAR
EL VAGÓN DE CARGA

WHEELBARROW
LA CARRETILLA

CAMCORDER
LA CÁMERA DE VÍDEO

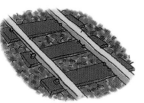

TRACK
LA VÍA

NEWSPAPER
EL PERIÓDICO

UMBRELLA
EL PARAGUAS

CART
EL CARRITO DE EQUIPAJE

Medios de transporte

BY LAND • POR TIERRA

CAR • **EL CARRO/EL COCHE**

RACE CAR • **EL CARRO DE CARRERAS**

VAN • **LA CAMIONETA**

AMBULANCE • **LA AMBULANCIA**

FIRE ENGINE •
EL CARRO DE BOMBEROS

MOTORCYCLE • **LA MOTO**

BUS • **EL AUTOBÚS**

TAXI • **EL TAXI**

TRAIN • **EL TREN**

TRUCK • **EL CAMIÓN**

TRACTOR • **EL TRACTOR**

EXCAVATOR • **LA EXCAVADORA**

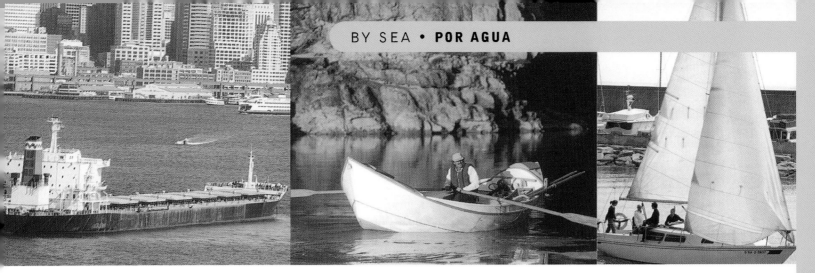

SHIP • **EL BARCO**   ROWBOAT • **EL BOTE DE REMOS**   SAILBOAT • **EL VELERO**

SPEEDBOAT • **LA LANCHA**   CANOE • **LA CANOA**   YACHT • **EL YATE**

BY AIR • **POR AIRE**

PLANE • **EL AVIÓN**   ROCKET • **EL COHETE**   LIGHT AIRCRAFT • **LA AVIONETA**

ULTRALIGHT • **EL ULTRALIGERO**   HOT-AIR BALLOON • **EL GLOBO**   HELICOPTER • **EL HELICÓPTERO**

TO STROLL **PASEAR**

TO GO UP **SUBIR**

TO GO DOWN **BAJAR**

TO WAIT **ESPERAR**

TO GO IN **ENTRAR**

TO GO OUT **SALIR**

TO OPEN **ABRIR**

TO CLOSE **CERRAR**

TO CROSS **CRUZAR**

TO SLIP **RESBALAR**

TO STUMBLE **TROPEZAR**

TO TALK ON THE PHONE **HABLAR POR TELÉFONO**

TO RIDE A BICYCLE **MONTAR EN BICICLETA**

TO TAKE OFF **DESPEGAR**

TO LAND **ATERRIZAR**

TO DRIVE **CONDUCIR**

TO BREATHE **RESPIRAR**

TO BLOW ONE'S NOSE **SOPLARSE LA NARIZ**

TO CURE **CURAR**

TO BANDAGE **VENDAR**

TO LAUGH **REÍR**

TO CRY **LLORAR**

TO SNEEZE **ESTORNUDAR**

TO COUGH **TOSER**

TO GUARD **VIGILAR**

TO LOAD **CARGAR**

TO UNLOAD **DESCARGAR**

TO WEIGH **PESAR**

TO SPEED UP **ACELERAR**

TO PASS **ADELANTAR**

TO TURN **VIRAR**

TO BRAKE **FRENAR**

TO CRASH **CHOCARSE**

TO TRAVEL **VIAJAR**

TO SAY GOOD-BYE **DESPEDIRSE**

What are they like?
¿Cómo es?, ¿cómo está?

OLD **ANTIGUO**

MODERN **MODERNO**

OPEN **ABIERTO**

CLOSED **CERRADO**

SWEET **DULCE**

SALTY **SALADO**

SOUR **ÁCIDO**

BITTER **AMARGO**

SPICY **PICANTE**

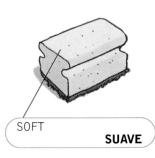

SOFT **SUAVE**

ROUGH **ÁSPERO**

SOLID **SÓLIDO**

LIQUID **LÍQUIDO**

THICK **GRUESA**

THIN **FINA**

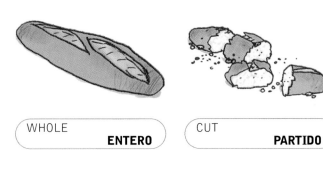

WHOLE **ENTERO**

CUT **PARTIDO**

RAW **CRUDAS**

FRIED **FRITAS**

UNRIPE **VERDE**

RIPE **MADURO**

SPOILED **ESTROPEADO**

66

HARD
DURO

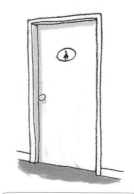

SOFT
BLANDO

WITH THE LID ON
TAPADO

WITH THE LID OFF
DESTAPADO

FREE
LIBRE

BUSY
OCUPADO

NERVOUS
NERVIOSA

CALM
TRANQUILA

HEALTHY
SANO

SICK
ENFERMO

INDUSTRIOUS
TRABAJADOR

LAZY
PEREZOSO

BORED
ABURRIDA

WITH A COLD
ACATARRADO

GREEDY
GOLOSA

CURIOUS
CURIOSO

RAINBOW **EL ARCO IRIS**

ISLAND **LA ISLA**

LIGHTHOUSE **EL FARO**

PEDAL BOAT **EL PATÍN**

BOAT **LA BARCA**

SEA **EL MAR**

WAVE **LA OLA**

SAND **LA ARENA**

SUNSCREEN **LA CREMA PROTECTORA**

SHELL **LA CONCHA**

CRAB **EL CANGREJO**

BUCKET **EL CUBO**

SHOVEL **LA PALA**

MOLD **EL MOLDE**

WATERING CAN **LA REGADERA**

SUNGLASSES **LAS GRAFAS DE SOL**

ICE-CREAM CONE **LA BARQUILLA**

ICE-CREAM POP **EL POLO**

INNER TUBE **EL FLOTADOR**

FLOATS **LOS MANGUITOS**

LIFE JACKET **EL CHALECO SALVAVIDAS**

CAP **LA GORRA**

GOGGLES **LAS GAFAS DE BUCEAR**

Going camping
De acampada

LEAVES
LAS HOJAS

BRANCH
LA RAMA

BIRDS
LOS PÁJA

BEEHIVE
EL PANAL

SNOW
LA NIEVE

BEE
LA ABEJA

TOWN
EL PUEBLO

MOUNTAIN
LA MONTAÑA

HAMMOCK
LA HAMACA

SMOKE
EL HUMO

FENCE
LA CERCA

CROPS
LOS CULTIVO

BOTTLE
LA GARRAFA

BARBECUE
LA BARBACOA

TENT
LA TIENDA DE CAMPAÑA

ROPE
LA SOGA

PENKNIFE
LA NAVAJA

STONE
LA PIEDRA

FISH

TWIG
EL PALO

RIVER
EL RÍO

MAGNIFYING GLASS
LA LUPA

BUNCH OF FLOWERS
EL RAMO DE FLORES

SPIDER'S WEB
LA TELARAÑA

SPIDER
LA ARAÑA

TREE
EL ÁRBOL

FISHING ROD
LA CAÑA DE PESCAR

FISHERMAN
EL PESCADOR

LAKE
EL LAGO

SHEPHERD
EL PASTOR

FLOCK OF SHEEP
EL REBAÑO

ANTS
LAS HORMIGAS

GRASS
LA HIERBA

DRAGONFLY
LA LIBÉLULA

NEST
EL NIDO

BONE
EL HUESO

LADYBUG
LA MARIQUITA

SNAIL
EL CARACOL

LIZARD
LA LAGARTIJA

BUTTERFLY
LA MARIPOSA

WATER BOTTLE
LA CANTIMPLORA

THERMOS
EL TERMO

CATERPILLAR
LA ORUGA

COMPASS
LA BRÚJULA

SCARECROW
EL ESPANTAPÁJAROS

At the fair
En la feria

PAPER LANTERN **EL FAROLILLO**

ROLLER COASTER **LA MONTAÑA RUSA**

FERRIS WHEEL **LA NORIA**

INFLATABLE CASTLE **EL CASTILLO HINCHABLE**

MERRY-GO-ROUND **EL TIOVIVO**

TRAILER **EL CARROMATO**

SINGER **EL CANTANTE**

MAGICIAN **EL MAGO**

SKELETON **EL ESQUELETO**

JUGGLER **EL MALABARISTA**

WIG **LA PELUCA**

CLOWN **EL PAYASO**

CAT **EL GATO**

FORTUNE-TELLER **LA ADIVINA**

BELL **EL CASCABEL**

CRYSTAL BALL **LA BOLA DE CRISTAL**

CANDLESTICKS **LAS PALMATORIAS**

MASK **LA CARETA**

SPACESHIP
LA NAVE ESPACIAL

PUPPET
LA MARIONETA

SURGICAL COLLAR
EL COLLARÍN

BUBBLE
LA BOMBA

TARGET SHOOTING
EL TIRO AL BLANCO

SOFT DRINK
EL REFRESCO

BULL'S-EYE
LA DIANA

DART
EL DARDO

TURBAN
EL TURBANTE

TOP HAT
EL SOMBRERO DE COPA

HAMBURGER
LA HAMBURGUESA

CANDY CANE
EL BASTÓN DE CARAMELO

COUPLE
LA PAREJA

HOT DOG
EL PERRITO CALIENTE

MICROPHONE
EL MICRÓFONO

POTATO CHIPS
LAS PAPAS FRITAS

POPCORN
LAS PALOMITAS

COTTON CANDY
EL ALGODÓN DE AZÚCAR

RACE DRIVER
EL PILOTO

FIREMAN
EL BOMBERO

PHOTOGRAPHER
LA FOTÓGRAFA

PAINTER
EL PINTOR

POLICEWOMAN
LA POLICÍA

BALLET DANCER
LA BAILARINA

MECHANIC
LA MECÁNICA

COWGIRL
LA VAQUERA

COWBOY
EL VAQUERO

COOK
LA COCINERA

SCIENTIST
EL CIENTÍFICO

ASTRONAUT
EL ASTRONAUTA

KNIGHT
EL CABALLERO

CAVEWOMAN
LA MUJER PREHISTÓRICA

SULTAN
EL SULTÁN

JESTER
EL BUFÓN

PIRATE
EL PIRATA

KING
EL REY

SOLDIER
EL SOLDADO

SUPERHERO
EL SUPERHÉROE

MOUSE
EL RATÓN

MUSKETEER
EL MOSQUETERO

ANGEL
EL ÁNGEL

DEVIL
EL DIABLO

TO PUT CREAM ON
PONERSE CREMA

TO SUNBATHE
TOMAR EL SOL

TO SHIVER
TIRITAR

TO MELT
DERRETIRSE

TO BUILD
CONSTRUIR

TO WATER
REGAR

TO TAKE A SHOWER
DUCHARSE

TO SPLASH
SALPICAR

TO FLOAT
FLOTAR

TO SINK
HUNDIRSE

TO DIVE
BUCEAR

TO WATCH
OBSERVAR

TO CAMP
ACAMPAR

TO POINT
SEÑALAR

TO SAIL
NAVEGAR

TO ROW
REMAR

TO WALK
ANDAR

TO RUN
CORRER

TO FLY
VOLAR

TO SLITHER
REPTAR

TO SUCKLE **MAMAR**

TO LICK **LAMER**

TO LICK **CHUPAR**

TO SCRATCH **ARAÑAR**

TO STING **PICAR**

TO ATTACK **ATACAR**

TO SNIFF **OLER**

TO CLIMB **ESCALAR**

TO FISH **PESCAR**

TO PAINT **PINTAR**

TO NAIL **CLAVAR**

TO MOW **SEGAR**

TO PRUNE **PODAR**

TO SAW **SERRAR**

TO DIG **CAVAR**

TO PLOW **ARAR**

TO BREAK UP **PICAR**

TO CHOP DOWN **TALAR**

TO SOW **SEMBRAR**

SUNNY **SOLEADO**

CLOUDY **NUBLADO**

NARROW **ESTRECHO**

WIDE **ANCHO**

FAST **RÁPIDA**

SLOW **LENTA**

CAUGHT **ATRAPADA**

FREE **LIBRE**

DIFFICULT **DIFÍCIL**

EASY **FÁCIL**

RESISTANT **RESISTENTE**

FRAGILE **FRÁGIL**

INFLATED **INFLADO**

DEFLATED **DESINFLADO**

FOLDED **DOBLADO**

STRETCHED **ESTIRADO**

ALIKE **IGUALES**

DIFFERENT **DISTINTOS**

PALE **PÁLIDA**

TAN **MORENA**

STRANGE **RARO**

NORMAL **NORMAL**

COWARDLY **COBARDE**

BRAVE **VALIENTE**

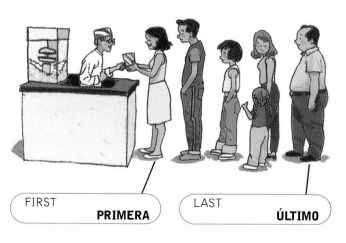

FIRST **PRIMERA**

LAST **ÚLTIMO**

WELL-MANNERED **EDUCADA**

BAD-MANNERED **MALEDUCADA**

DOMESTIC **DOMÉSTICO**

WILD **SALVAJE**

TAME **MANSO**

FIERCE **FEROZ**

Good morning. What's your name?
My name is Anne.

Buenos días. ¿Cómo te llamas?
Me llamo Ana.

Good afternoon. How are you?
I'm very good, thank you.

Buenas tardes. ¿Cómo estás?
Estoy muy bien, gracias.

How old is the baby?
He's one. Happy birthday!

¿Cuántos años tiene el bebé?
El tiene un año. ¡Feliz cumpleaños!

What is today's date?
Today is the 4th of July.

¿Cuál es la fecha?
Hoy es el cuatro de Julio.

I'm cold!

¡Tengo frío!

I'm sick.

Estoy enfermo.

Helen is thirsty.

Elena tiene sed.

I'm scared.

Tengo miedo.

Are you hot?
No, I'm tired.

¿Tienes calor?
No, tengo sueño.

How is Christine?
She's sad.

¿Cómo está Cristina?
Ella está triste.

The sisters are happy.

Las hermanas están contentas.

The friends are happy, too.

Los amigos están contentos también.

It's sunny.

Hace sol.

It's raining. See you later!

Está lloviendo. ¡Hasta la vista!

What are you wearing?
I'm wearing shoes.

¿Qué llevas?
Llevo los zapatos.

What color is your skirt?
My skirt is purple.

¿Qué color es tu falda?
Mi falda es morada.

What is Mary doing?
She's jumping rope.

¿Qué hace Maria?
Ella salta la cuerda.

What are you doing, George?
I'm throwing the ball.

¿Qué haces, Jorge?
Tiro el balón.

What is Robert doing?
He's eating because he is hungry.

¿Qué hace Roberto?
El come por que tiene hambre.

Who is kissing the boy?
The girl is kissing the boy.

¿Quién besa al muchacho?
La muchacha besa al muchacho.

Who is holding the book?
The teacher is holding the book.

¿Quién tiene el libro?
La profesora tiene el libro.

Where are you?
I'm inside the house.

¿Donde estás?
Estoy dentro de la casa.

Look right. Look left.

Now cross the street.

Mira a la derecha. Mira a la izquierda.
Y ahora cruza la calle.

Here comes the bus. Where are you going?
I'm going to school.

Aquí viene el autobús. ¿Adónde vas?
Voy a la escuela.

What are you going to do?
I'm going to play soccer.

¿Qué vas a hacer?
Voy a jugar al fútbol.

Look at the pronunciation guide in parentheses after each Spanish word or expression in this word list. It will teach you to pronounce the Spanish words and phrases as Spanish speakers do. When you pronounce the guides out loud, read them as you would read words and syllables in English.

Here are a few hints about saying words in Spanish. The Spanish "r" is different from the English "r." To say it correctly, "trill" the sound by flapping your tongue against the roof of your mouth once. Whenever you see "rr" in the pronunciation guide, trill the sound longer by flapping your tongue several times. The Spanish letter "ñ" is pronounced "ny." You will see it written as "ny" in the pronunciation guides. The letter "ll" is pronounced as "y" and that's how you will see it in the pronunciation. The letter "a" always sounds like the "a" in "father." The letter "o" always sounds like the "o" in "go." And always pronounce the letter "e" as in "let."

Each word in the pronunciation guides has one syllable in bold letters. This is the stressed syllable. When you read the pronunciation aloud, just say the bold syllable a little louder than the others to use the correct stress.

a través de (a tra-**behs** deh) through 51
abajo (a-**ba**-ho) down 51
el abecedario (el a-beh-seh-**da**-ryo) alphabet 31
la abeja (la a-**beh**-ha) bee 70
abierto (a-**byer**-toh) open 26, 66
abrazar (a-bra-**sar**) to hug 24
el abrigo (el a-**bree**-go) coat 23
abril (a-**breel**) April 32
abrir (a-**breer**) to open 64
abrochado (a-bro-**cha**-doh) buttoned 26
abrochar (a-bro-**char**) to button 49
la abuela (la a-**bweh**-la) grandmother 6
el abuelo (el a-**bweh**-lo) grandfather 6
aburrida (a-boor-**ree**-da) bored 67
la acampada (la a-cam-**pa**-da) camping 70
acampar (a-cam-**par**) to camp 76
acariciar (a-ca-ree-**syar**) to pet 24
acatarrado (a-ca-ta-**rra**-doh) with a cold 67
acelerar (a-seh-leh-**rar**) to speed up 65
la acelgas (la a-**sel**-gas) chard 10
la acera (la a-**seh**-ra) sidewalk 53
ácido (a-**see**-doh) sour 66
la acomodadora (la a-co-mo-da-**dor**-a) usher 40
el acordeón (el a-kor-deh-**on**) accordion 43
acostarse (a-co-**star**-seh) to go to bed 25
actuar (ac-too-**ar**) to perform 49
las acuarelas (las aqua-**reh**-las) watercolors 28
adelantar (a-deh-**lan**-tar) to pass 65
la adivina (la a-dee-**bee**-na) fortune-teller 72
afeitarse (a-feh-**tar**-seh) to shave 25
agosto (a-**go**-sto) August 32
el agua (el **a**-gwa) water 34
el aguacate (el a-gwa-**ka**-teh) avocado 11
el aire (el **eh**-reh) air 63
el ajedrez (el a-heh-**dres**) chess 55
el ajo (el **a**-ho) garlic 10
al lado de (al **la**-do deh) next to 51
el ala delta (el **a**-la **del**-ta) hang gliding 39
la alacena (la a-la-**seh**-na) hutch 15
el albaricoque (el al-ba-ree-**ko**-keh) apricot 11
el álbum (el **al**-boom) binder 29; album 35
la alcachofa (la al-ka-**cho**-fa) artichoke 10
la alcancía (la al-can-**see**-ya) piggy bank 21
la alcantarilla (la al-can-ta-**ree**-ya) drain 52
el alcohol (el al-**col**) alcohol 58
la alfombra (la al-**fom**-bra) rug 13
la alfombrilla (la al-fom-**bree**-ya) mousepad 13
las alforjas (las al-**for**-has) saddlebag 45
el algodón (el al-go-**dohn**) cotton 59

el algodón de azúcar (el al-go-**dohn** deh a-**soo**-kar) cotton candy 73
los alicates (los a-lee-**ka**-tes) pliers 13
las almendras (las al-**mehn**-dras) almonds 10
la almohada (la al-mo-**ah**-da) pillow 20
alrededor (al-reh-deh-**dor**) around 51
alta (**al**-ta) tall 50
los altavoces (los al-ta-**bo**-ses) loudspeakers 60
alumbrar (a-loom-**brar**) to light 49
los alumnos (los a-**loom**-nohs) students 28
amargo (a-**mar**-go) bitter 66
el amarillo (el a-ma-**ree**-yo) yellow 30
la ambulancia (la am-boo-**lan**-sya) ambulance 62
los anacardos (los a-na-**kar**-dohs) cashew nuts 10
ancho (**an**-cho) wide 78
anciano (an-**sya**-no) old 50
andar (an-**dar**) to walk 76
el andén (el an-**dehn**) platform 61
el ángel (el **an**-hel) angel 75
las anillas (las a-**nee**-yas) rings 37
los animales (los a-nee-**ma**-les) animals 46
el antebrazo (el an-teh-**bra**-so) forearm 19
antiguo (an-**tee**-gwo) old 66
el anular (el a-noo-**lar**) ring finger 19
apagada (a-pa-**ga**-da) off 26
el aparador (el a-pa-ra-**dor**) sideboard 15
la araña (la a-**ra**-nya) spider 71
arañar (a-ra-**nyar**) to scratch 77
arar (a-**rar**) to plow 77
el árbol (el **ar**-bol) tree 71
el arco iris (el **ar**-ko **ee**-rees) rainbow 69
la arena (la a-**reh**-na) sand 69
el armario (el ar-**ma**-ree-o) armoire 15
la armónica (la ar-**mo**-nee-ka) harmonica 43
el aro (el **a**-ro) hoop 37
arrastrar (a-rras-**trar**) to drag 49
arriba (a-**ree**-ba) up 51
arrugada (a-rroo-**ga**-da) wrinkled 26
las artes marciales (las **ar**-tes mar-**sya**-les) martial arts 39
el asiento (el a-**syen**-toh) seat 59
áspero (**as**-peh-ro) rough 66
la aspiradora (la as-pee-ra-**doh**-ra) vacuum 12
el astronauta (el as-tro-**now**-ta) astronaut 74
atacar (a-ta-**kar**) to attack 77
atar (a-**tar**) to tie up 49
atenta (a-**tehn**-ta) attentive 50
aterrizar (a-tehr-ree-**sar**) to land 64
atrapada (a-tra-**pa**-da) caught 78
el autobús (el ow-toh-**boos**) bus 62

las avellanas (las a-beh-**ya**-nas) hazelnuts 10
la avería (la a-beh-**ree**-a) breakdown 52
el avión (el a-**byon**) plane 63
la avioneta (la a-byo-**neh**-ta) light aircraft 63
la azada (la a-**sa**-da) hoe 45
el azucarero (el a-soo-ka-**reh**-ro) sugar bowl 9
el azul claro (el **a**-sool **kla**-ro) light blue 30
el azul oscuro (el **a**-sool o-**scoo**-ro) dark blue 30

el babero (el ba-**beh**-ro) bib 8
la bailarina (la bigh-la-**ree**-na) ballet dancer 74
baja (**ba**-ha) short 50
bajar (ba-**har**) to go down 64
el bajón (ba-**hon**) bassoon 43
el balancín (el ba-lan-**seen**) rocking horse 55
la balanza (la ba-**lan**-sa) scales 57
los balcones (los bal-**kon**-ehs) balconies 52
las baldosas (las bal-**doh**-sas) tiles 16
el balón (el ba-**lon**) ball 34
el baloncesto (el ba-lon-**ses**-toh) basketball 38
el balonmano (el ba-lon-**ma**-no) handball 38
la banana (la ba-**na**-na) banana 11
bañarse (ba-**nyar**-seh) to take a bath 25
el banco (el **ban**-ko) stool 16; bench 52; bank 53
la bandeja (la ban-**deh**-ha) tray 8
la bandera (la ban-**deh**-ra) flag 53
el banderín (el ban-deh-**reen**) banner 57
la bañera (la ba-**nyeh**-ra) bath 16
el banjo (el **ban**-ho) banjo 42
el banquillo (el ban-**kee**-yo) ottoman 14
la barandilla (la ba-ran-**dee**-ya) banister 35
la barba (la **bar**-ba) beard 40
la barbacoa (la bar-ba-**ko**-a) barbecue 70
la barbilla (la bar-**bee**-ya) chin 19
la barca (la **bar**-ka) boat 69
el barco (el **bar**-ko) ship 63
la barquilla (la bar-**kee**-ya) ice-cream cone 69
la barra (la **ba**-rra) bar 9
barrer (ba-**rrehr**) to sweep 25
la barrera (la ba-**rreh**-ra) barrier 61
el barril (el ba-**rreel**) barrel 45
la báscula (la **bas**-koo-la) scale 16
el bastón (el bas-**ton**) walking stick 40
el bastón de caramelo (el bas-**ton** deh ca-ra-**meh**-lo) candy cane 73

los **bastoncillos** (los bas-ton-**see**-yos) cotton swabs 17
la **bata** (la **ba**-ta) bathrobe 16; housecoat 21
la **batería** (la ba-teh-**ree**-ya) drum set 42
la **batidora** (la ba-tee-**doh**-ra) blender 9
batir (ba-**teer**) to whisk 24
el **baúl** (el ba-**ool**) trunk 20
el **bebé** (el beh-**beh**) baby 6
beber (beh-**ber**) to drink 24
el **béisbol** (el behs-**bol**) baseball 38
besar (beh-**sar**) to kiss 24
el **biberón** (el bee-beh-**ron**) bottle 21
la **bicicleta** (la bee-see-**kleh**-ta) bicycle 54
el **bidé** (el bee-**deh**) bidet 16
el **bigote** (el bee-**go**-teh) moustache 40
la **billetera** (la bee-yeh-**teh**-ra) wallet 57
el **blanco** (el **blan**-ko) white 30
blando (**blan**-do) soft 67
la **boca** (la **bo**-ka) mouth 19
la **bocina** (la bo-**see**-na) speaker 13
la **bola** (la **bo**-la) ball 41
la **bola de cristal** (la **bo**-la deh kree-**stal**) crystal ball 72
el **bolígrafo** (el bo-**lee**-gra-fo) pen 29
los **bolos** (los **bo**-los) bowling 55
la **bolsa** (la **bol**-sa) bag 6
el **bolso** (el **bol**-so) purse 57
la **bomba** (la **bom**-ba) bubble 73
el **bombero** (el bom-**beh**-ro) fireman 74
el **borrador** (el bo-rra-**dor**) eraser 29
borrar (bo-**rrar**) to erase 48
bostezar (bos-teh-**sar**) to yawn 25
botar (bo-**tar**) to bounce 49
las **botas** (las **bo**-tas) boots 23
el **bote de remos** (el **bo**-teh deh **reh**-mos) rowboat 63
la **botella** (la bo-**teh**-ya) bottle 7
los **botes** (los **bo**-tehs) jars 29
el **botiquín** (el bo-tee-**keen**) medicine cabinet 16
el **botón** (el bo-**ton**) button 21
el **brazo** (el **bra**-so) arm 18
los **brotes** (los **bro**-tehs) shoots 28
la **bruja** (la **broo**-ha) witch 41
la **brújula** (la **broo**-hoo-la) compass 71
bucear (boo-seh-**ar**) to dive 76
la **bufanda** (la boo-**fan**-da) scarf 57
el **bufón** (el boo-**fon**) jester 75
el **burro** (el **boo**-rro) donkey 45
la **butaca** (la boo-**ta**-ka) armchair 14
las **butacas** (las boo-**ta**-kas) seats 40
el **buzón** (el boo-**son**) mailbox 53

el **caballero** (el ka-ba-**yeh**-ro) knight 75
el **caballete** (el ka-ba-**yeh**-teh) easel 29
el **caballo** (el ka-**ba**-yo) horse 44
la **cabeza** (la ka-**beh**-sa) head 19
la **cabina telefónica** (la ka-**bee**-na teh-leh-**fo**-nee-ka) phone booth 53
la **cabra** (la **ka**-bra) goat 44
los **cacauetes** (los ka-ka-**wa**-tes) peanuts 10
el **cachorro** (el ka-**cho**-rro) puppy 45
el **cactus** (el **kak**-toos) cactus 13
la **cadena** (la ka-**deh**-na) chain 41
la **cafetera** (la ka-feh-**teh**-ra) coffeemaker 9
la **caja china** (la **ka**-ha **chee**-na) Chinese box 42
la **caja de herramientas** (la **ka**-ha deh eh-rra-**myen**-tas) toolbox 13
la **caja registradora** (la **ka**-ha reh-hees-tra-**doh**-ra) cash register 55
la **cajera** (la ka-**heh**-ra) cashier 57
el **cajero automático** (el ka-**heh**-ro ow-toh-**ma**-tee-ko) ATM 53
el **cajón** (el ka-**hon**) drawer 21

el **calabacín** (el ka-la-ba-**seen**) zucchini 10
la **calabaza** (la ka-la-**ba**-sa) pumpkin 10
la **calavera** (la ka-la-**beh**-ra) skull 58
los **calcetines** (los kal-seh-**tee**-nes) socks 22
el **calentador** (el ka-len-ta-**dor**) water heater 9
caliente (ka-**lyen**-teh) hot 26
la **calzada** (la kal-**sa**-da) road 53
calzado (kal-**sa**-doh) with shoes on 27
los **calzoncillos** (los kal-son-**see**-yos) underpants 22
la **cama** (la **ka**-ma) bed 15
la **cama elástica** (la **ka**-ma eh-**las**-tee-ka) trampoline 37
la **cámara de fotos** (la **ka**-ma-ra deh **fo**-tos) camera 60
la **cámara de vídeo** (la **ka**-ma-ra deh **bee**-deh-o) camcorder 61
el **camello** (el ka-**meh**-yo) camel 47
la **camilla** (la ka-**mee**-ya) stretcher 58
el **camino** (el ka-**mee**-no) path 41
el **camión** (el ka-**myon**) truck 62
la **camioneta** (la ka-myo-**neh**-ta) van 62
la **camisa** (la ka-**mee**-sa) shirt 22
la **camiseta** (la ka-mee-**seh**-ta) T-shirt 22
el **camisón** (el ka-mee-**son**) nightgown 21
la **campana extractora** (la kam-**pa**-na ex-trak-**toh**-ra) range hood 8
la **campanilla** (la kam-pa-**nee**-ya) uvula 19; handbell 40
la **caña de pescar** (la **ka**-nya deh **pehs**-kar) fishing rod 71
la **canasta** (la ka-**nas**-ta) basket 34
el **candelabro** (el kan-deh-**la**-bro) candleholder 12
la **cañería** (la ka-nya-**ree**-ya) pipe 34
el **cangrejo** (el kan-**greh**-ho) crab 69
el **canguro** (el kan-**goo**-ro) kangaroo 47
las **canicas** (las ka-**nee**-kas) marbles 34
la **canoa** (la ka-**no**-a) canoe 63
cansada (kan-**sa**-da) tired 50
el **cantante** (el kan-**tahn**-teh) singer 72
la **cantimplora** (la kan-teem-**plo**-ra) water bottle 71
el **caracol** (el ka-ra-**kol**) snail 71
la **careta** (la ka-**reh**-ta) mask 7, 72
cargar (kar-**gar**) to load 65
la **carne** (la **kar**-neh) meat 56
el **carnero** (el kar-**neh**-ro) ram 44
la **carnicería** (la kar-nee-seh-**ree**-a) butcher's 56
el **carnicero** (el kar-nee-**seh**-ro) butcher 56
la **carpeta** (la kar-**peh**-ta) folder 21
la **carrera** (la ka-**rreh**-ra) race 39
la **carretilla** (la ka-rreh-**tee**-ya) wheelbarrow 61
el **carrito de equipaje** (el ka-**rree**-toh deh eh-kee-**pa**-heh) cart 61
el **carro** (el **ka**-rro) shopping cart 57; car 62
el **carro de bomberos** (el **ka**-rro deh bom-**beh**-ros) fire engine 62
el **carro de carreras** (el **ka**-rro deh ka-**rreh**-ras) race car 62
el **carro de limpieza** (el **ka**-rro deh leem-**pyeh**-sa) cleaner's cart 60
el **carromato** (el ka-rro-**ma**-toh) trailer 72
las **cartas** (las **kar**-tas) cards 34
el **cartel** (el kar-**tel**) sign 59
la **carterita** (la kar-teh-**ree**-ta) coin purse 57
el **cartero** (el kar-**teh**-ro) mail carrier 53
el **cartón** (el kar-**ton**) carton 8
el **cascabel** (el **kas**-ka-bel) bell 72
el **casco** (el **kas**-ko) helmet 53
las **castañuelas** (las kas-ta-nyoo-**weh**-los) castanets 42
el **castillo** (el kas-**tee**-yo) castle 68

el **castillo hinchable** (el kas-**tee**-yo een-**cha**-bleh) inflatable castle 72
cavar (ka-**bar**) to dig 77
el **cazo** (el **ka**-so) saucepan 8
la **cazuela** (la ka-**sweh**-la) casserole 9
el **CD** (el **seh**-deh) CD 13
la **cebolla** (la seh-**bo**-ya) onion 10
la **cebra** (la **seh**-bra) zebra 46
la **ceja** (la **seh**-ha) eyebrow 19
el **celular** (el seh-loo-**lar**) mobile phone 53
el **cementerio** (el seh-men-**teh**-ryo) cemetery 41
el **cencerro** (el sen-**seh**-rro) bell 45
cepillar (seh-pee-**yar**) to brush 25
el **cepillo** (el seh-**pee**-yo) broom 12; hairbrush 17
el **cepillo de dientes** (el seh-**pee**-yo deh **dyen**-tes) toothbrush 17
el **cepillo de uñas** (el seh-**pee**-yo deh **oo**-nyas) nailbrush 17
cerca (**ser**-ka) near 51
la **cerca** (la **ser**-ka) fence 70
el **cerdo** (el **ser**-do) pig 45
los **cereales** (los seh-reh-**a**-les) cereal 8
la **cereza** (la seh-**reh**-sa) cherry 7
cerrado (seh-**rra**-doh) closed 26, 66
cerrar (seh-**rrar**) to close 64
la **cesta** (la **ses**-ta) laundry basket 12; basket 57
el **chaleco** (el cha-**leh**-ko) vest 22
el **chaleco salvavidas** (el cha-**leh**-ko sal-ba-**bee**-das) life jacket 69
el **champú** (el cham-**poo**) shampoo 16
las **chanclas** (las **chan**-clas) flip-flops 68
el **chándal** (el **chan**-dal) tracksuit 36
la **chaqueta** (la cha-**keh**-ta) cardigan 22; jean jacket 23
la **charca** (la **char**-ka) pond 45
el **charco** (el **char**-ko) puddle 52
la **chimenea** (la chee-meh-**neh**-a) chimney 45
el **chimpancé** (el cheem-pan-**seh**) chimpanzee 47
chocarse (cho-**car**-seh) to crash 65
la **chorrera** (la cho-**rreh**-ra) slide 52
chupar (choo-**par**) to lick 77
el **chupete** (el choo-**peh**-teh) pacifier 21
el **ciclismo** (el see-**clees**-mo) cycling 38
el **científico** (el syen-**tee**-fee-ko) scientist 74
cinco (**seen**-ko) five 33
el **cine** (el **see**-neh) movie theater 52
la **cinta** (la **seen**-ta) ribbon 36
la **cintura** (la seen-**too**-ra) waist 19
el **círculo** (el **seer**-koo-lo) circle 30, 35
el **clarinete** (el kla-ree-**neh**-teh) clarinet 43
clavar (kla-**bar**) to nail 77
los **clavos** (los **kla**-bos) nails 13
cobarde (ko-**bar**-deh) coward 79
el **coche** (el **ko**-cheh) car 53
el **coche teledirigido** (el **ko**-cheh teh-leh-dee-ree-**hee**-doh) remote-controlled car 21
el **cochecito** (el ko-cheh-**see**-toh) car 55
la **cocina** (la ko-**see**-na) kitchen 8
cocinar (ko-see-**nar**) to cook 24
la **cocinera** (la ko-see-**neh**-ra) cook 74
el **coco** (el **ko**-ko) coconut 11
el **código de barras** (el **ko**-dee-go deh **ba**-rras) bar code 57
el **codo** (el **ko**-do) elbow 19
el **cohete** (el ko-**eh**-teh) rocket 63
el **cojín** (el ko-**heen**) cushion 12
el **colador** (el ko-la-**dor**) strainer 9
la **colcha** (la **kol**-cha) bedspread 20
el **colchón** (el kol-**chon**) mattress 20
la **colchoneta** (la kol-cho-**neh**-ta) mat 36; air bed 68
la **coleta** (la ko-**leh**-ta) ponytail 34

el collar (el ko-**yar**) necklace 35
el collarín (el ko-ya-**reen**) surgical collar 73
la colonia (la ko-**lo**-nya) cologne 16
colorear (ko-lo-reh-**ar**) to color 48
los colores (los co-**lo**-res) colors 30
la comba (la **kom**-ba) jump rope 34
comer (ko-**mer**) to eat 24
la cometa (la ko-**meh**-ta) kite 68
la cómoda (la **ko**-mo-da) dresser 15
cómoda (**ko**-mo-da) comfortable 27
la computadora (la kom-poo-ta-**doh**-ra) computer 13
la concha (la **kon**-cha) shell 69
conducir (kon-doo-**seer**) to drive 64
el conductor (el kon-dook-**tor**) engine driver 60
la conductora (la kon-dook-**toh**-ra) driver 53
el conejo (el ko-**neh**-ho) rabbit 44
las congas (las **kon**-gahs) conga drums 42
los congelados (los kon-heh-**la**-dos) frozen food 57
las conservas (las kon-**ser**-bas) canned food 57
la consigna (la kon-**seeg**-na) luggage 61
las construcciones (las kons-trook-**syo**-nehs) Lego bricks 54
construir (kon-stroo-**eer**) to build 76
contar (kon-**tar**) to count 48
el contenedor (el kon-teh-neh-**dor**) container 57
contento (kon-**ten**-toh) happy 27
el contrabajo (el kon-tra-**ba**-ho) double bass 42
el corazón (el kor-a-**sohn**) heart 30, 58
los cordones (los kor-**doh**-nes) laces 21
la corneta (la kor-**neh**-ta) cornet 43
la corona (la ko-**ro**-na) crown 7
el correo (el ko-**rreh**-o) post office 52
correr (ko-**rrer**) to run 76
cortar (kor-**tar**) to cut 48
cortarse las uñas (kor-**tar**-seh las **oo**-nyas) to cut one's nails 25
la cortina (la kor-**tee**-na) curtain 9
corto (**kor**-toh) short 50
coser (ko-**ser**) to sew 49
la crema protectora (la **kreh**-ma pro-tec-**toh**-ra) sunscreen 69
la cremallera (la kreh-ma-**yeh**-ra) zipper 21
los crines (los **kree**-nehs) mane 44
el cronómetro (el kro-**no**-meh-tro) stopwatch 37
los crótalos (los **kro**-ta-los) small cymbals 41
crudas (**kroo**-das) raw 66
cruzar (kroo-**sar**) to cross 64
la cuadra (la **kwa**-dra) stable 44
el cuadrado (el kwa-**dra**-doh) square 30
los cuadros (los **kwa**-dros) paintings 12
cuarto (**kwar**-toh) fourth 33
el cuarto de baño (el **kwar**-toh deh **ba**-nyo) bathroom 16
el cuarto de estar (el **kwar**-toh deh es-**tar**) living room 12
cuatro (**kwa**-tro) four 33
el cubo (el **koo**-bo) cube 37; bucket 69
la cuchara (la koo-**cha**-ra) spoon 9
la cucharilla (la koo-cha-**ree**-ya) teaspoon 9
el cuchillo (el koo-**chee**-yo) knife 9
el cuello (el **kweh**-yo) neck 19
el cuento (el **kwen**-toh) storybook 21
la cuerda de nudos (la **kwer**-da deh **noo**-dos) rope 36
el cuerpo (el **kwer**-po) body 18
los cultivos (los kool-**tee**-bos) crops 70
la cuna (la **koo**-na) crib 15, 20

curar (koo-**rar**) to cure 65
curioso (koo-**ryo**-so) curious 67

las damas (las **da**-mas) checkers 55
dar una patada (dar **oon**-a pa-**ta**-da) to kick 49
dar una voltereta (dar **oon**-a bol-teh-**reh**-ta) to turn somersaults 49
el dardo (el **dar**-doh) dart 73
de pie (deh pyeh) standing 50
debajo (deh-**ba**-ho) under 51
débil (**deh**-beel) weak 50
décimo (**deh**-see-mo) tenth 33
los dedos (los **deh**-dohs) fingers 19
el del corazón (el del ko-ra-**sohn**) middle finger 19
el delantal (el deh-lan-**tal**) apron 56
delante (deh-**lan**-teh) in front of 51
delgado (del-**ga**-doh) thin 50
dentro (**den**-tro) in 51
los deportes (los deh-**por**-tes) sports 38
derretirse (deh-rreh-**teer**-seh) to melt 76
desabrochado (des-a-bro-**cha**-doh) unbuttoned 26
desabrochar (des-a-bro-**char**) to unbutton 49
desatar (des-a-**tar**) to untie 49
descalzo (des-**kal**-so) barefoot 27
el descapotable (el des-ka-po-**ta**-bleh) convertible 68
descargar (des-kar-**gar**) to unload 65
desde (**des**-deh) from 51
desenvolver (des-en-bol-**ber**) to unwrap 48
desinflado (des-een-**fla**-doh) deflated 78
el desodorante (el des-o-dor-**ahn**-teh) deodorant 17
desordenado (des-or-deh-**na**-doh) messy 26
despedirse (des-peh-**deer**-seh) to say good-bye 65
despegar (des-peh-**gar**) to take off 64
despeinado (des-peh-**na**-doh) uncombed 27
el despertador (el des-per-ta-**dor**) alarm clock 21
despierto (des-**pyer**-toh) awake 27
destapado (des-ta-**pa**-doh) with the lid off 67
el destornillador (el des-tor-nee-ya-**dor**) screwdriver 13
desvestido (des-bes-**tee**-doh) undressed 27
detrás (deh-**tras**) behind 51
el diablo (el dee-**a**-blo) devil 75
la diadema (la dee-a-**deh**-ma) headband 35
la diana (la dee-**a**-na) bull's-eye 73
los días (los **dee**-as) days 32
dibujar (dee-boo-**har**) to draw 48
los dibujos (los dee-**boo**-hos) drawings 29
diciembre (dee-**syem**-breh) December 32
los dientes (los **dyen**-tehs) teeth 19
diez (dyes) ten 33
difícil (dee-**fee**-seel) difficult 78
el dinosaurio (el dee-no-**sahw**-ryo) dinosaur 21
los disfraces (los dees-**fra**-sehs) costumes 74
distintos (dees-**teen**-tohs) different 79
distraída (dees-tra-**yee**-da) distracted 50
el diván (el dee-**ban**) divan 14
doblado (doh-**bla**-doh) folded 78
la doctora (la doc-tor-**a**) doctor 58
doméstico (doh-**mes**-tee-ko) domestic 79
el domingo (el doh-**meen**-go) Sunday 32
el dominó (el doh-mee-**no**) dominoes 54
dormido (dor-**mee**-doh) asleep 27
dormir (dor-**meer**) to sleep 25
el dormitorio (el dor-mee-**toh**-ryo) bedroom 20
dos (dohs) two 33
el dragón (el dra-**gon**) dragon 40

el dromedario (el dro-meh-**da**-ryo) dromedary 47
la ducha (la **doo**-cha) shower 16
ducharse (doo-**char**-seh) to take a shower 76
el duende (el **dwen**-deh) elf 41
dulce (**dool**-seh) sweet 66
duro (**doo**-ro) hard 67

el edredón (el ed-reh-**don**) comforter 20
educada (eh-doo-**ka**-da) well-mannered 79
el elefante (el eh-leh-**fan**-teh) elephant 46
empujar (em-poo-**har**) to push 49
en cuclillas (en koo-**clee**-yas) squatting 50
encendida (en-sen-**dee**-da) on 26
el enchufe (el en-**choo**-feh) socket 13
encima (en-**see**-ma) on 51
enero (eh-**neh**-ro) January 32
la enfermera (la en-fer-**meh**-ra) nurse 58
enfermo (en-**fer**-mo) sick 67
enfrente (en-**fren**-teh) opposite 51
entero (en-**teh**-ro) whole 66
entrar (en-**trar**) to go in 64
entre (**en**-treh) between 51
envolver (en-bol-**behr**) to wrap 48
el equipo de música (el eh-**kee**-po deh **moo**-see-ka) stereo 13
la escala (la es-**ka**-la) window ladder 36
la escalada (la es-ka-**la**-da) climbing 39
escalar (es-ka-**lar**) to climb 77
la escalera (la es-ka-**leh**-ra) ladder 20
la escalera de incendios (la es-ka-**leh**-ra deh een-**sen**-dyos) fire escape 53
el escenario (el eh-seh-**na**-ryo) stage 40
la escoba (la es-**ko**-ba) broom 41
esconderse (es-kon-**der**-seh) to hide 49
el escondite (el es-**kon**-dee-teh) hide-and-seek 34
escribir (es-kree-**beer**) to write 48
el escritorio (el es-kree-**toh**-ryo) desk 15
escuchar (es-koo-**char**) to listen 48
el escurreplatos (el es-koo-reh-**pla**-tos) plate rack 9
la esgrima (la **es**-gree-ma) fencing 39
la espada (la es-**pa**-da) sword 41
la espalda (la es-**pal**-da) back 19
las espalderas (las es-pal-**deh**-ras) wall bars 36
el espantapájaros (el es-pan-ta-**pa**-ha-ros) scarecrow 71
el esparadrapo (el es-pa-ra-**dra**-po) medical tape 58
los espárragos blancos (los es-**pa**-rra-gos **blan**-kos) white asparagus 10
los espárragos trigueros (los es-**pa**-rra-gos tree-**ger**-os) green asparagus 10
el especiero (el es-peh-**syer**-o) spice rack 8
los espectadores (los es-pek-ta-**doh**-res) spectators 40
el espejo (el es-**peh**-ho) mirror 17
esperar (es-peh-**rar**) to wait 64
la espinilla (la es-pee-**nee**-ya) shin 19
la esponja (la es-**pohn**-ha) sponge 17
el esqueleto (el es-keh-**leh**-toh) skeleton 72
el esquí (el es-**kee**) skiing 38
la esquina (la es-**kee**-na) corner 12
el establo (el es-**ta**-blo) barn 44
la estación de tren (la es-ta-**syon** deh tren) train station 60
las estaciones (las es-ta-**syon**-ehs) seasons 32
estirado(-a) (es-tee-**ra**-doh[-da]) ironed 26; stretched 78
estirarse (es-tee-**rar**-seh) to stretch 25
el estómago (el es-**toh**-ma-go) stomach 58
el estor (el es-**tohr**) roller blind 6
estornudar (es-tor-noo-**dar**) to sneeze 65

estrecho (es-**treh**-cho) narrow 78
la estrella (la es-**treh**-ya) star 30
estropeado (es-tro-peh-**ya**-doh) spoiled 66
el estuche (el es-**too**-cheh) case 28
la excavadora (la es-ka-ba-**dor**-a) excavator 62
la excursión (la es-koor-**syon**) trip 44
explicar (es-plee-**kar**) to explain 48
el exprimidor (el es-pree-mee-**dor**) juicer 9
el extintor (el es-teen-**tor**) fire extinguisher 37

fácil (**fa**-seel) easy 78
la falda (la **fal**-da) skirt 22
la familia (la fa-**mee**-lya) family 6
el fantasma (el fan-**tas**-ma) ghost 40
el faro (el **fa**-ro) lighthouse 69
el farol (el fa-**rol**) lamppost 53
el farolillo (el fa-ro-lee-yo) paper lantern 72
febrero (feh-**breh**-ro) February 32
feo (**feh**-oh) ugly 50
feroz (feh-**ros**) fierce 79
la fila (la **fee**-la) line 34
fina (**fee**-na) thin 66
la flauta andina (la **flaoo**-ta an-**dee**-na) panpipes 43
la flauta dulce (la **flaoo**-ta **dool**-seh) recorder 43
la flauta travesera (la **flaoo**-ta tra-beh-**seh**-ra) flute 43
los flecos (los **fleh**-kos) tassles 13
el flexo (el **flex**-o) reading lamp 20
el flotador (el flo-ta-**dor**) inner tube 69
flotar (flo-**tar**) to float 76
el fluorescente (el floo-or-es-**en**-teh) fluorescent light 37
los focos (los **fo**-cos) spotlights 40
el fonendoscopio (el fo-nen-doh-**sco**-pyo) stethoscope 59
las formas (las **for**-mas) shapes 30
los fósforos (los **fos**-fo-ros) matches 7
la fotógrafa (la fo-**toh**-gra-fa) photographer 74
la fotografía (la fo-toh-gra-**fee**-a) photograph 28
las fotos (las **fo**-tos) pictures 35
frágil (**fra**-heel) fragile 78
los frascos (los **fras**-kos) jars 8
el fregadero (el freh-ga-**deh**-ro) sink 9
la freidora (la freh-ee-**doh**-ra) fryer 9
frenar (freh-**nar**) to brake 65
la frente (la **fren**-teh) forehead 19
la fresa (la **freh**-sa) strawberries 11
frío (**free**-o) cold 26
fritas (**free**-tas) fried 66
la fruta (la **froo**-ta) fruit 56
la frutería (la froo-teh-**rya**) fruit stall 56
los frutos (los **froo**-tos) fruit 10
la fuente (la **fwen**-teh) water fountain 34
fuera (**fwe**-ra) out 51
fuerte (**fwer**-teh) strong 50
el fútbol (el **fooht**-bol) soccer 38

las gafas (las **ga**-fas) glasses 35
las gafas de bucear (las **ga**-fas deh boo-**seh**-ar) goggles 69
las gafas de sol (las **ga**-fas deh sol) sunglasses 69
las galletas (las ga-**yeh**-tas) cookies 35
las gallinas (las ga-**yee**-nas) hens 44
el gallo (el **ga**-yo) rooster 45
el gancho (el **gan**-cho) hanger 21
la garrafa (la ga-**rra**-fa) pitcher 70
la gasa (la **ga**-sa) gauze bandage 58

la gasolinera (la ga-so-lee-**neh**-ra) gas station 68
el gato (el **ga**-toh) cat 72
el gazapo (el ga-**sa**-po) bunny 44
el gel (el hel) shower gel 16
el gimnasio (el heem-**na**-syo) gym 36
el globo (el **glo**-bo) hot-air balloon 63
los globos (los **glo**-bos) balloons 6
el golf (el golf) golf 38
golosa (go-**lo**-sa) greedy 67
la goma (la **go**-ma) eraser 29
gordo (**gor**-doh) fat 50
el gorila (el go-**ree**-la) gorilla 47
la gorra (la **go**-rra) cap 69
el gorro (el **go**-rro) hat 23, 57
el granate (el gra-**na**-teh) maroon 30
grande (**gran**-deh) big 26
la granja (la **gran**-ha) farm 44
el granjero (el gran-**heh**-ro) farmer 44
el grifo (el **gree**-fo) faucet 17
el gris (el grees) gray 30
gruesa (groo-**eh**-sa) thick 66
los guantes (los **gwan**-tes) gloves 57
guapo (**gwa**-po) good-looking 50
los guisantes (los gee-**san**-tes) peas 10
la guitarra (la gee-**ta**-rra) guitar 42
la guitarra eléctrica (la gee-**ta**-rra eh-**lek**-tree-ka) electric guitar 42
gustar (goos-**tar**) to taste 24

hablar (a-**blar**) to speak 48
hablar por teléfono (a-**blar** por teh-**leh**-fo-no) to talk on the phone 64
hacer la cama (a-**ser** la **ka**-ma) to make one's bed 25
el hacha (el **a**-cha) axe 45
hacia (**a**-sya) toward 51
el hada (el **a**-da) fairy 40
la hamaca (la a-**ma**-ka) hammock 70
la hamburguesa (la am-boor-**geh**-sa) hamburger 73
hasta (**as**-ta) to 51
el helicóptero (el eh-lee-**kop**-teh-ro) helicopter 63
la herida (la eh-**ree**-da) injury 58
la hermana (la er-**ma**-na) sister 6
el hermano (el er-**ma**-no) brother 6
el hielo (el **ye**-lo) ice 7
la hierba (la **yer**-ba) grass 71
la hípica (la **ee**-pee-ka) horseback riding 38
el hipopótamo (el ee-po-**po**-ta-mo) hippopotamus 46
el hockey (el **ho**-kee) hockey 38
la hoja (la **o**-ha) sheet of paper 28
las hojas (las **o**-has) leaves 70
el hombro (el **om**-bro) shoulder 19
las hormigas (las or-**mee**-gahs) ants 71
el horno (el **or**-no) oven 8
la horquilla (la or-**kee**-ya) barrette 35
el hotel (el o-**tel**) hotel 52
el hoyo (el **oy**-o) hole 68
las huellas (las **weh**-yas) footprints 68
el hueso (el **weh**-so) bone 71
el humo (el **oo**-mo) smoke 70
hundirse (oon-**deer**-seh) to sink 76

la iglesia (la ee-**gleh**-sya) church 52
iguales (ee-**gwa**-lehs) alike 79
el imán (el ee-**man**) magnet 9
el impermeable (el eem-per-meh-**a**-bleh) raincoat 23
incómoda (een-**ko**-mo-da) uncomfortable 27
el índice (el **een**-dee-seh) index finger 19
inflado (een-**fla**-doh) inflated 78

la información (la een-for-ma-**syon**) information desk 60
el inodoro (el ee-no-**doh**-ro) toilet 16
los instrumentos con teclado (los een-stroo-**men**-tohs kon teh-**kla**-doh) keyboard instruments 43
los instrumentos de cuerda (los een-stroo-**men**-tohs deh **kwer**-da) string instruments 42
los instrumentos de percusión (los een-stroo-**men**-tohs deh per-koo-**syon**) percussion instruments 42
los instrumentos de viento (los een-stroo-**men**-tohs deh **byen**-toh) wind instruments 43
los instrumentos musicales (los een-stroo-**men**-tohs moo-see-**ka**-lehs) musical instruments 42
el interruptor (el een-teh-rroop-**tohr**) switch 13
el invierno (el een-**byer**-no) winter 32
la isla (la **ees**-la) island 69

el jabón (el ha-**bon**) soap 17
el jarabe (el ha-ra-beh) syrup 59
la jardinera (la har-dee-**neh**-ra) window box 35
el jardinero (el har-dee-**neh**-ro) gardener 34
la jarra (la **ha**-rra) pitcher 7
el jarrón (el ha-**rron**) vase 12
la jeringuilla (la heh-reen-**gee**-ya) syringe 59
el jersey (el **her**-seh) sweater 22
la jirafa (la hee-**ra**-fa) giraffe 46
joven (**ho**-ben) young 50
las judías verdes (las hoo-**dee**-as **ber**-dehs) beans 10
el juego electrónico (el **hweh**-go eh-lek-**tro**-nee-ka) electronic game 55
los juegos (los **hweh**-gos) games 54
el jueves (el **hweh**-bes) Thursday 32
jugar (hoo-**gar**) to play 48
el jugo (el **hoo**-go) juice 8
los juguetes (los hoo-**geh**-tes) toys 54
julio (hoo-**lyo**) July 32
junio (hoo-**nyo**) June 32

el kiwi (el **kee**-wee) kiwi 11
el koala (el ko-**wa**-la) koala 47

los labios (los **la**-byos) lips 19
la lagartija (la la-gar-**tee**-ha) lizard 71
el lago (el **la**-go) lake 71
lamer (la-**mehr**) to lick 77
la lámpara (la **lam**-pa-ra) lamp 12
la lancha (la **lan**-cha) speedboat 63
el lápiz (el **la**-pees) pencil 29
largo (**lar**-go) long 50
el lavabo (el la-**ba**-bo) sink 17
la lavadora (la la-ba-**dor**-a) washing machine 9
el lavaplatos (el la-ba-**pla**-tohs) dishwasher 9
lavar los platos (la-**bar** los **pla**-tohs) to wash 24
lavarse (la-**bar**-seh) to wash oneself 25
el lazo (el **la**-so) ribbon 35
el lechón (el leh-**chon**) piglet 45
la lechuga (la leh-**choo**-ga) lettuce 10
leer (leh-**er**) to read 48
lejos (**leh**-hos) far 51
la leña (la **leh**-nya) firewood 45
la lengua (la **len**-gwa) tongue 19
lenta (**len**-ta) slow 78
el león (el leh-**on**) lion 46

el leopardo (el leh-o-**par**-doh) leopard 46

los leotardos (los leh-o-**tar**-dohs) tights 22

las letras (las **leh**-tras) letters 28

levantarse (leh-ban-**tar**-seh) to get up 25

la libélula (la lee-**beh**-loo-la) dragonfly 71

libre (**lee**-breh) free 67, 78

el librero (el lee-**breh**-ro) bookcase 15

el libro (el **lee**-bro) book 13

el limón (el lee-**mon**) lemon 11

limpia (**leem**-pya) clean 27

la limpiadora (la leem-pya-**doh**-ra) cleaner 60

limpiar (leem-**pyar**) to clean 25

el lince (el **leen**-seh) lynx 46

la linterna (la leen-**ter**-na) flashlight 41

líquido (**lee**-kee-do) liquid 66

liso (**lee**-so) straight 50

la llama (la **ya**-ma) llama 46

la llanta (la **yan**-ta) tire 53

la llave (la **ya**-beh) key 13

el llavero (el ya-**beh**-ro) key ring 13

lleno (**yeh**-no) full 26

llorar (yo-**rar**) to cry 65

la luna (la **loo**-na) moon 40

el lunes (el **loo**-nes) Monday 32

la lupa (la **loo**-pa) magnifying glass 70

la maceta (la ma-**seh**-ta) flowerpot 35

la madre (la **ma**-dreh) mother 6

maduro (ma-**doo**-ro) ripe 66

el mago (el **ma**-go) magician 72

el malabarista (el ma-la-ba-**rees**-ta) juggler 72

maleducada (mal-eh-doo-**ka**-da) bad-mannered 79

la maleta (la ma-**leh**-ta) suitcase 60

la malla (la **ma**-ya) leotard 36

mamar (ma-**mar**) to suckle 77

la mampara (la **mam**-pa-ra) partition 16

mancharse (man-**char**-seh) to get dirty 25

el mango (el **man**-go) mango 11

la manguera (la man-**geh**-ra) hose 34

los manguitos (los man-**gee**-tohs) floats 69

la mano (la **ma**-no) hand 18

las manoplas (las ma-**no**-plas) mittens 57

manso (**man**-so) tame 79

la manta (la **man**-ta) blanket 20

el mantel (el man-**tel**) tablecloth 6

la manzana (la man-**sa**-na) apple 11

el mapa (el **ma**-pa) map 28

maquillar (ma-kee-**yar**) to make up 49

el mar (el mar) sea 69

las maracas (las ma-**ra**-kas) maracas 42

el marco (el **mar**-ko) frame 12

la marioneta (la ma-ree-o-**neh**-ta) puppet 73

la mariposa (la ma-ree-**po**-sa) butterfly 71

la mariquita (la ma-ree-**kee**-ta) ladybug 71

el marrón (el ma-**rron**) brown 30

el martes (el **mar**-tes) Tuesday 32

el martillo (el mar-**tee**-yo) hammer 13

marzo (**mar**-so) March 32

la mascarilla (la mas-ka-**ree**-ya) mask 58

el matasuegras (el ma-ta-**sweh**-gras) noisemaker 7

la matrícula (la ma-**tree**-koo-la) license plate 53

mayo (**ma**-yo) May 32

la maza (la **ma**-sa) club 36

la mecánica (la meh-**ka**-nee-ka) mechanic 74

la mecedora (la meh-seh-**doh**-ra) rocking chair 14

la medalla (la meh-**da**-ya) medal 35

la medialuna (la meh-dya-**loo**-na) half moon 30

las medicinas (las meh-dee-**see**-nas) medicine 58

los medios (los **meh**-dyos) means 62

el melocotón (el meh-lo-ko-**tohn**) peach 11

el melón (el meh-**lon**) melon 11

el meñique (el meh-**nyee**-keh) pinky 19

la mermelada (la mer-meh-**la**-da) jam 9

la mesa camilla (la **meh**-sa ka-**mee**-ya) round table 14

la mesa de comedor (la **meh**-sa deh ko-meh-**dor**) dining table 14

la mesa de despacho (la **meh**-sa deh des-**pa**-cho) desk 14

los meses (los **meh**-ses) months 32

la mesilla (la meh-**see**-ya) nightstand 21

el metro (el **meh**-tro) subway 53

el micrófono (el mee-**kro**-fo-no) microphone 73

el microondas (el mee-kro-**on**-das) microwave 8

el miércoles (el **myer**-ko-lehs) Wednesday 32

las migas (las **mee**-gas) crumbs 52

la mochila (la mo-**chee**-la) backpack 28

modelar (mo-**deh**-lar) to shape 48

moderno (mo-**der**-no) modern 66

mojada (mo-**ha**-da) wet 27

el molde (el **mol**-deh) mold 69

el molino (el mo-**lee**-no) windmill 44

las monedas (las mo-**neh**-das) coins 57

el monopatín (el mo-no-pa-**teen**) skateboard 54

el monstruo (el **mon**-stro) monster 40

la montaña (la mon-**ta**-nya) mountain 70

la montaña rusa (la mon-**ta**-nya **roo**-sa) roller coaster 72

el montañismo (el mon-ta-**nyees**-mo) hiking 39

montar en bicicleta (mon-**tar** en bee-see-**kleh**-ta) to ride a bicycle 64

el monumento (el mo-noo-**men**-toh) memorial 52

el morado (el mo-**ra**-doh) purple 30

morena (mo-**reh**-na) tan 79

el mosquetero (el mos-keh-**teh**-ro) musketeer 75

el mostrador (el mos-tra-**dor**) counter 56

la moto (la **mo**-toh) motorcycle 62

la moto acuática (la **mo**-toh a-**kwa**-tee-ka) jet ski 68

los muebles (los **mweh**-blehs) furniture 14

las muelas (las **mweh**-las) molars 19

la mujer prehistórica (la **moo**-hehr preh-ees-**toh**-ree-ka) cavewoman 75

la muleta (la moo-**leh**-ta) crutch 35

la muñeca (la moo-**nyeh**-ka) wrist 19; doll 55

el muñeco (el moo-**nyeh**-ko) doll 21

el murciélago (el moor-**syeh**-la-go) bat 41

los musculos (los **moos**-koo-los) muscles 58

el muslo (el **moos**-lo) thigh 19

el nabo (el **na**-bo) turnip 10

el naranja (el na-**ran**-ha) orange (color) 30

la naranja (la na-**ran**-ha) orange (fruit) 11

la nariz (la na-**rees**) nose 19

la natación (la na-ta-**syon**) swimming 38

la navaja (la na-**ba**-ha) penknife 70

la nave espacial (la **na**-beh es-pa-**syal**) spaceship 73

navegar (na-beh-**gar**) to sail 76

el negro (el **neh**-gro) black 30

nerviosa (nehr-**byo**-sa) nervous 67

la nevera (la neh-**beh**-ra) fridge 9

el nido (el **nee**-doh) nest 71

la nieve (la **nyeh**-beh) snow 70

la niña (la **nee**-nya) girl 29

el niño (el **nee**-nyo) boy 29

el níspero (el **nees**-peh-ro) medlar 11

la noria (la **no**-rya) Ferris wheel 72

normal (nor-**mal**) normal 79

noveno (no-**beh**-no) ninth 33

noviembre (no-**byem**-breh) November 32

la nube (la **noo**-beh) cloud 68

nublado (noo-**bla**-doh) cloudy 78

los nudillos (los noo-**dee**-yos) knuckles 19

las nueces (las **nweh**-ses) walnuts 11

nueve (**nweh**-beh) nine 33

nuevo (**nweh**-bo) new 26

los números (los **noo**-meh-ros) numbers 33

el oboe (el o-**bo**-eh) oboe 43

el obrero (el o-**breh**-ro) worker 61

observar (ob-ser-**bar**) to watch 76

la oca (la **o**-ka) goose 45

ocho (**o**-cho) eight 33

el ocre (el **o**-kreh) ochre 30

octava (ok-**ta**-ba) eighth 33

octubre (ok-**too**-breh) October 32

ocupado (o-koo-**pa**-doh) busy 67

la oficina (la o-fee-**see**-na) office 58

oír (o-**eer**) to listen 24

el ojal (el o-**hal**) buttonhole 21

los ojos (los **o**-hos) eyes 19

la ola (la **o**-la) wave 69

oler (o-**ler**) to smell 24; to sniff 77

el ombligo (el om-**blee**-go) belly button 18

la óptica (la **op**-tee-ka) optician's 53

el orangután (el o-ran-goo-**tan**) orangutan 47

ordenado (or-deh-**na**-doh) neat 26

la oreja (la o-**reh**-ha) ear 19

el órgano (el **or**-ga-no) organ 43

el orinal (el o-ree-**nal**) potty 17

la oruga (la o-**roo**-ga) caterpillar 71

el oso de peluche (el **o**-so deh peh-**loo**-cheh) teddy bear 54

el oso panda (el **o**-so **pan**-da) panda bear 47

el oso pardo (el **o**-so **par**-doh) brown bear 47

el oso polar (el **o**-so po-**lar**) polar bear 47

el otoño (el o-**toh**-nyo) autumn/fall 32

el óvalo (el **o**-ba-lo) oval 30

la oveja (la o-**beh**-ha) sheep 45

el ovillo (el o-**bee**-yo) ball 29

el paciente (el pa-**syen**-teh) patient 58

el padre (el **pa**-dreh) father 6

el paisaje (el paee-**sa**-heh) landscape 12

el pajar (el pa-**har**) hayloft 45

los pájaros (los **pa**-ha-ros) birds 70

la pala (la **pa**-la) shovel 69

el paladar (el pa-la-**dar**) palate 19

pálida (**pa**-lee-da) pale 79

los palillos (los pa-**lee**-yos) toothpicks 7

las palmatorias (las pal-ma-**toh**-ryas) candlesticks 72

el palo (el **pa**-lo) twig 70

las palomas (las pa-**lo**-mas) pigeons 52

las palomitas (las pa-lo-**mee**-tas) popcorn 73

el panal (el **pa**-nal) beehive 70

el pañal (el pa-**nyal**) diaper 20

la pandereta (la pan-deh-**reh**-ta) tambourine 41, 42

el panel de información (el **pa**-nel deh een-for-ma-**syon**) information board 60

las pantaletas (las pan-ta-**leh**-tas) panties 22

la pantalla (la pan-**ta**-ya) screen 13

el pantalón corto (el pan-ta-**lon kor**-toh) shorts 23

el pantalón de peto (el pan-ta-**lon** deh **peh**-toh) overalls 23

el pantalón largo (el pan-ta-**lon lar**-go) pants 23

la pantera (la pan-**teh**-ra) panther 46

la pantorrilla (la pan-toh-**rree**-ya) calf 19

el pañuelo (el pa-**nyweh**-lo) scarf 57

los pañuelos de papel (los pa-**nyweh**-los deh **pa**-pel) tissues 17

la papa (la **pa**-pa) potato 10

las papas fritas (las **pa**-pas **free**-tas) potato chips 73

el papel celo (el **pa**-pel **seh**-lo) tape 29

el papel de cocina (el **pa**-pel deh ko-**see**-na) paper towels 9

el papel higiénico (el **pa**-pel ee-**hyeh**-nee-ko) toilet paper 16

la papelera (la pa-peh-**leh**-ra) wastepaper bin 29

el parachoques (el pa-ra-**cho**-kehs) bumper 53

la parada de autobús (la pa-**ra**-da deh ow-toh-**boos**) bus stop 52

el paraguas (el pa-**ra**-gwas) umbrella 61

las paralelas (las pa-ra-**leh**-las) parallel bars 37

el parchís (el par-**chees**) Parcheesi 55

la pared (la pa-**red**) wall 13

la pareja (la pa-**reh**-ha) couple 73

el párpado (el **par**-pa-do) eyelid 19

el parque (el **par**-keh) park 52

las partes (las **par**-tehs) parts 18

partido (par-**tee**-doh) cut 66

partir (par-**teer**) to break 24

las pasas (las **pa**-sas) raisins 11

pasear (pa-seh-**ar**) to stroll 64

la pasta de dientes (la **pa**-sta deh **dyen**-tehs) toothpaste 17

los pasteles (los pa-**steh**-lehs) cakes 53

las pastillas (las pas-**tee**-yas) pills 59

el pastor (el pa-**stor**) shepherd 71

el patín (el pa-**teen**) pedal boat 69

el patinaje (el pa-tee-**na**-heh) skating 38

los patines (los pa-**tee**-nehs) skates 54

el patinete (el pa-tee-**neh**-teh) scooter 54

el pato (el **pa**-toh) duck 44

el pavo (el **pa**-bo) turkey 45

el pehaso (el pa-**ya**-so) clown 72

el pecho (el **peh**-cho) breast/chest 18

la pega (la **peh**-ga) glue 29

pegar (peh-**gar**) to glue 48

peinado (peh-**na**-do) combed 27

peinarse (peh-**nar**-seh) to comb one's hair 25

el peine (el **peh**-neh) comb 17

pelar (peh-**lar**) to peel 24

la pelota (la peh-**lo**-ta) ball 21

la peluca (la peh-**loo**-ka) wig 72

pequeño (peh-**keh**-nyo) small 26

la pera (la **peh**-ra) pear 11

el perchero (el per-**cheh**-ro) clothes rack 28

perezoso (peh-reh-**so**-so) lazy 67

el perfume (el per-**foo**-meh) perfume 16

la perilla (la peh-**ree**-ya) goatee 40

el periódico (el peh-**ryo**-dee-ko) newspaper 61

el perrito caliente (el peh-**rree**-toh ka-**lyen**-teh) hot dog 73

el perro (el **peh**-rro) dog 45

la persiana (la per-**sya**-na) blinds 12

pesar (peh-**sar**) to weigh 65

la pescadera (la pes-ka-**deh**-ra) fishmonger 56

el pescado (el pes-**ka**-doh) fish 56

el pescador (el pes-ka-**dor**) fisherman 71

pescar (pes-**kar**) to fish 77

el pesebre (el peh-**seh**-breh) trough 44

las pestañas (las peh-**sta**-nyas) eyelashes 19

el pez (el pes) fish 70

el piano (el **pya**-no) piano 43

la pica (la **pee**-ka) pike 36

picante (pee-**kan**-teh) spicy 66

picar (pee-**kar**) to sting; to break up 77

el pichi (el **pee**-chee) jumper 22

el pico (el **pee**-ko) pick 61

el pie (el pyeh) foot 18

la piedra (la **pyeh**-dra) stone 70

la pierna (la **pyer**-na) leg 18

el pijama (el pee-**ha**-ma) pajama 20

el piloto (el pee-**lo**-toh) race driver 74

el pimiento rojo (el pee-**myen**-toh **ro**-ho) red pepper 10

el pimiento verde (el pee-**myen**-toh **ber**-deh) green pepper 10

la piña (la **pee**-nya) pineapple 11

el pincel (el peen-**sel**) paintbrush 29

el ping-pong (el peen-**pon**) ping-pong 39

el pintalabios (el peen-ta-**la**-byos) lipstick 17

pintar (peen-**tar**) to paint 77

el pintor (el peen-**tor**) painter 74

las pinturas (las peen-**too**-ras) paints 28

el piragüismo (el pee-ra-**gwees**-mo) canoeing 39

el pirata (el pee-**ra**-ta) pirate 75

los pistachos (los pee-**sta**-chos) pistachio nuts 10

el pitillo (el pee-**tee**-yo) drinking straw 6

la pizarra (la pee-**sa**-rra) blackboard 29

la plancha (la **plan**-cha) iron 13

planchar (plan-**char**) to iron 25

la planta (la **plan**-ta) plant 6

la plastilina (la plas-tee-**lee**-na) clay 29

el plato (el **pla**-toh) plate 9

la playa (la **pla**-ya) beach 68

el plinto (el **pleen**-toh) vaulting box 37

la pluma (la **ploo**-ma) feather 41

el plumero (el ploo-**meh**-ro) feather duster 13

la pocilga (la po-**seel**-ga) pigsty 44

podar (po-**dar**) to prune 77

la policía (la po-lee-**see**-a) policewoman 74

los pollos (los **poy**-yos) chicks 44

el polo (el **po**-lo) knitted shirt 22; ice-cream pop 69

el polvo de talco (el **pol**-bo deh **tal**-ko) talcum powder 17

la pomada (la po-**ma**-da) ointment 59

ponerse crema (po-**ner**-seh **kreh**-ma) to put cream on 76

la portería (la por-teh-**rya**) goal 34

el portero (el por-**teh**-ro) goalie 34

el póster (el **po**-stehr) poster 20

el potro (el **po**-tro) vaulting horse 37; pony 44

la primavera (la pree-ma-**beh**-ra) spring 32

primera (pree-**meh**-ra) first 33, 79

el primo (el **pree**-mo) cousin 7

el príncipe (el **preen**-see-peh) prince 41

los prismáticos (los prees-**ma**-tee-kos) binoculars 61

la profesora (la pro-feh-**so**-ra) teacher 28

el pueblo (el **pweh**-blo) town 70

el puente (el **pwen**-teh) bridge 68

el puenting (el pwen-**teen**) bungee jumping 39

el puerro (el **pweh**-rro) leek 10

la puerta (la **pwer**-ta) door 12

el pulgar (el pool-**gar**) thumb 19

el pulmón (el pool-**mon**) lung 58

la pulsera (la pool-**seh**-ra) bracelet 35

el puma (el **poo**-ma) puma 46

quinta (**keen**-ta) fifth 33

el quiosco (el **kyo**-sko) kiosk 68

el radio (el **rra**-dyo) radio 16

el radiocasete (el rra-dyo-ka-**seh**-teh) radio cassette 21

la radiografía (la rra-dyo-gra-**fya**) x-ray 58

el rafting (el **rraf**-teen) rafting 39

el raíl (el rra-**eel**) rail 61

la rama (la **rra**-ma) branch 70

el ramo de flores (el **rra**-mo deh **flo**-rehs) bunch of flowers 70

la rampa (la **rram**-pa) ramp 35

rápida (**rra**-pee-da) fast 78

la raqueta (la rra-**keh**-ta) racket 20

raro (**rra**-ro) strange 79

el rastrillo (el rras-**tree**-yo) razor 17; rake 45

el ratón (el rra-**tohn**) mouse 13, 75

el rayo (el **rra**-yo) bolt of lightning 41

el rebaño (el rreh-**ba**-nyo) flock of sheep 71

el recogedor (el rreh-ko-heh-**dor**) dustpan 13

recostada (rreh-ko-**sta**-da) lying 50

el rectángulo (el rrek-**tan**-goo-lo) rectangle 30

recto (**rrek**-toh) straight 26

el redil (el rreh-**deel**) pen 44

el refresco (el rreh-**fres**-ko) soft drink 73

la regadera (la rreh-ga-**deh**-ra) watering can 69

regalar (rreh-ga-**lar**) to give a present 24

el regalo (el rreh-**ga**-lo) present 6

regar (rreh-**gar**) to water 76

la regla (la **rreh**-gla) ruler 29

reír (rreh-**eer**) to laugh 65

el reloj (el rreh-**lo**) clock 6

el reloj de pulsera (el rreh-**lo** deh pool-**seh**-ra) watch 37

remar (rreh-**mar**) to row 76

reptar (rrehp-**tar**) to slither 76

resbalar (rres-ba-**lar**) to slip 64

resistente (rreh-see-**sten**-teh) resistant 78

respirar (rrehs-pee-**rar**) to breathe 65

el retrato (el rreh-**tra**-toh) portrait 12

el revisor (el rreh-bee-**sor**) collector 60

el rey (el rreh) king 75

las riendas (las **rryen**-das) reins 45

el rinoceronte (el rree-no-seh-**ron**-teh) rhino 46

el río (el **rree**-o) river 70

rizado (rree-**sa**-doh) curly 50

el robot (el rro-**bot**) robot 20

el rociador (el rro-see-ya-**dor**) spray bottle 13

la rodilla (la rro-**dee**-ya) knee 19

la rodillera (la rro-dee-**yeh**-ra) knee pad 36

el rodillo (el rro-**dee**-yo) rolling pin 9

el rojo (el **rro**-ho) red 30

el rompecabezas (el rrom-peh-ka-**beh**-sas) (jigsaw) puzzle 54

la ropa (la **rro**-pa) clothes 22

la rosa (la **rro**-sa) pink 30

la rosquilla (la rros-**kee**-ya) doughnut 7

el rotulador (el rro-too-la-**dor**) marker 29

la rueda (la **rrweh**-da) wheel 53

el rugby (el **rroog**-bee) rugby 38

el sábado (el **sa**-ba-do) Saturday 32

la sábana (la **sa**-ba-na) sheet 20

el **sacapuntas** (el sa-ka-**poon**-tas) pencil sharpener 29

sacar punta (sa-**kar poon**-ta) to sharpen 48

el **saco** (el **sa**-ko) sack 61

la **sala de espera** (la **sa**-la deh es-**peh**-ra) waiting room 59

salado (sa-**la**-doh) salty 66

el **salero** (el sa-**leh**-ro) saltshaker 7

la **salida** (la sa-**lee**-da) exit 40

salir (sa-**leer**) to go out 64

salpicar (sal-pee-**kar**) to splash 76

saltar (sal-**tar**) to jump 49

el **salto de altura** (el **sal**-toh deh al-**too**-ra) high jump 39

el **salto de longitud** (el **sal**-toh deh lon-hee-**tood**) long jump 39

el **salto de vallas** (el **sal**-toh deh **ba**-yas) hurdle jump 39

saludar (sa-loo-**dar**) to greet 49

salvaje (sal-**ba**-heh) wild 79

el **salvavidas** (el sal-ba-**bee**-das) lifeguard 68

las **sandalias** (las san-**da**-lyas) sandals 23

la **sandía** (la san-**dee**-a) watermelon 11

el **sándwich** (el **san**-weesh) sandwich 7

sano (**sa**-no) healthy 67

el **sapo** (el **sa**-po) toad 45

el **sartén** (el sar-**ten**) frying pan 9

el **saxofón** (el sa-gso-**fon**) saxophone 43

seca (**seh**-ka) dry 27

el **secador** (el seh-ka-**dor**) hair dryer 17

secarse (seh-**kar**-seh) to dry oneself 25

segar (seh-**gar**) to mow 77

segunda (seh-**goon**-da) second 33

seis (sehs) six 33

el **semáforo** (el seh-**ma**-fo-ro) traffic light 53

la **semana** (la seh-**ma**-na) week 32

sembrar (sem-**brar**) to sow 77

la **señal de tráfico** (la seh-**nyal** deh tra-**fee**-ko) road sign 53

señalar (seh-nya-**lar**) to point 76

sentada (sen-**ta**-da) seated 50

separar (seh-pa-**rar**) to separate 48

septiembre (sep-**tyem**-breh) September 32

séptimo (**sep**-tee-mo) seventh 33

la **serpentina** (la ser-pen-**tee**-na) paper streamer 6

la **serpiente** (la ser-**pyen**-teh) snake 47

serrar (seh-**rrar**) to saw 77

los **servicios** (los ser-**bee**-syos) bathrooms 59

la **servilleta** (la ser-bee-**yeh**-ta) napkin 6

servir (ser-**beer**) to serve 24

la **seta** (la **seh**-ta) mushroom 40

sexta (**ses**-ta) sixth 33

siete (**syeh**-teh) seven 33

el **silbato** (el seel-**ba**-to) whistle 35

la **silla** (la **see**-ya) chair 14

la **silla de montar** (la **see**-ya deh mon-**tar**) saddle 45

la **silla de playa** (la **see**-ya deh **pla**-ya) deck chair 68

la **silla de ruedas** (la **see**-ya deh **rrweh**-das) wheelchair 34

la **silla plegable** (la **see**-ya pleh-**ga**-bleh) folding chair 68

la **sillita** (la see-**yee**-ta) stroller 57

el **sillón** (el see-**yon**) armchair 14

el **snowboard** (el sno-**bord**) snowboarding 39

el **sofá** (el so-**fa**) sofa 14

la **soga** (la **so**-ga) rope 70

el **sol** (el sol) sun 68

el **soldado** (el sol-**da**-doh) soldier 75

soleado (so-leh-**a**-doh) sunny 78

sólido (**so**-lee-doh) solid 66

soltar (sol-**tar**) to let go of 49

el **sombrero de copa** (el som-**breh**-ro deh **ko**-pa) top hat 73

la **sombrilla** (la som-**bree**-ya) beach umbrella 68

el **sonajero** (el so-na-**heh**-ro) rattle 21

soplar (so-**plar**) to blow 24

soplarse la nariz (so-**plar**-seh la na-**rees**) to blow one's nose 65

la **sortija** (la sor-**tee**-ha) ring 35

suave (**swa**-beh) soft 66

subir (soo-**beer**) to go up 64

sucia (**soo**-sya) dirty 27

sudar (soo-**dar**) to sweat 49

el **sudor** (el soo-**dor**) sweat 36

sujetar (soo-heh-**tar**) to hold 49

el **sultán** (el sool-**tan**) sultan 75

el **superhéroe** (el soo-per-**eh**-ro-eh) superhero 75

el **supermercado** (el soo-per-mer-**ka**-doh) supermarket 56

el **surtidor** (el soor-tee-**dor**) gas pump 68

la **tabla de planchar** (la **ta**-bla deh plan-**char**) ironing board 12

la **tabla para cortar** (la **ta**-bla **pa**-ra kor-**tar**) cutting board 8

tachar (ta-**char**) to cross out 48

el **taladro** (el ta-**la**-dro) drill 13

talar (ta-**lar**) to chop down 77

el **talón** (el ta-**lon**) heel 19

el **tambor** (el tam-**bor**) drum 42

la **tapa** (la **ta**-pa) lid 8

tapado (ta-**pa**-doh) with the lid on 67

el **tapón** (el ta-**pon**) plug 17

el **taxi** (el **ta**-gsee) taxi 62

la **taza** (la **ta**-sa) cup 9

el **tazón** (el ta-**sohn**) bowl 8

el **teatro** (el teh-**a**-tro) theater 40

el **techo** (el **teh**-cho) ceiling 12

el **teclado** (el teh-**kla**-doh) keyboard 13

la **telaraña** (la teh-la-**ra**-nya) spider's web 71

el **televisor** (el teh-leh-bee-**sor**) television 12

el **telón** (el teh-**lon**) curtain 41

las **tenazas** (las teh-**na**-sas) pincers 13

tender (ten-**der**) to hang up 25

el **tenedor** (el teh-neh-**dor**) fork 9

el **tenis** (el **teh**-nees) tennis 38

tercero (ter-**seh**-ro) third 33

el **termo** (el **ter**-mo) thermos 71

el **termómetro** (el ter-**mo**-meh-tro) thermometer 59

el **ternero** (el ter-**neh**-ro) calf 45

el **tesoro** (el teh-**so**-ro) treasure 40

la **tía** (la **tee**-a) aunt 7

el **tiempo** (el **tyem**-po) time 32

la **tienda** (la **tyen**-da) store 52

la **tienda de campaña** (la **tyen**-da deh kam-**pa**-nya) tent 70

la **tierra** (la **tyeh**-rra) land 62

el **tigre** (el **tee**-greh) tiger 46

las **tijeras** (las tee-**heh**-ras) scissors 29

el **timbal** (el teem-**bal**) kettle drum 42

el **tío** (el-**tee**-o) uncle 6

el **tiovivo** (el tee-o-**bee**-bo) merry-go-round 72

la **tira cómica** (la **tee**-ra **ko**-mee-ka) comic 35

el **tirador** (el tee-ra-**dor**) knob 17

tirar (tee-**rar**) to throw 49

la **tirita** (la tee-**ree**-ta) Band-Aid 58

tiritar (tee-ree-**tar**) to shiver 76

el **tiro al blanco** (el **tee**-ro al **blan**-ko) target shooting 74

los **títeres** (los **tee**-teh-rehs) puppets 55

las **tizas** (las **tee**-sas) pieces of chalk 28

la **toalla** (la toh-**a**-ya) towel 17

el **tobillo** (el toh-**bee**-yo) ankle 18

el **tocadiscos** (el toh-ka-**dees**-kos) record player 13

el **tocador** (el toh-ka-**dor**) dressing table 15

tocar (toh-**kar**) to touch 24

tocar un instrumento (toh-**kar** oon een-stroo-**men**-toh) to play an instrument 48

el **toldo** (el **tol**-doh) awning 53

tomar el sol (toh-**mar** el sol) to sunbathe 76

el **tomate** (el toh-**ma**-teh) tomato 10

torcido (tor-**see**-doh) crooked 26

el **toro** (el **toh**-ro) bull 45

la **toronja** (la toh-**ron**-ha) grapefruit 11

la **torre** (la **toh**-rreh) tower 68

la **torta** (la **tor**-ta) cake 6

la **tortuga** (la tor-**too**-ga) tortoise 47

toser (toh-**ser**) to cough 65

la **tostada** (la tos-**ta**-da) toast 8

la **tostadora** (la tos-ta-**doh**-ra) toaster 9

trabajador (tra-ba-ha-**dor**) industrious 67

el **tractor** (el trak-**tor**) tractor 62

el **traje de baño de niña** (el **tra**-heh deh **ba**-nyo deh **nee**-nya) swimsuit 23

el **traje de baño de niño** (el **tra**-heh deh **ba**-nyo deh **nee**-nyo) swimming trunks 23

el **trampolín** (el tram-po-**leen**) springboard 37

tranquila (tran-**kee**-la) calm 67

el **transporte** (el trans-**por**-teh) transportation 62

trapear (tra-peh-**ar**) to mop 25

el **trapo** (el **tra**-po) cloth 12

el **tren** (el tren) train 62

las **trenzas** (las **tren**-sas) braids 35

tres (tres) three 33

el **triángulo** (el tree-**an**-goo-lo) triangle 30, 41

el **triciclo** (el tree-**see**-clo) tricycle 54

triste (**trees**-teh) sad 27

el **trombón** (el trom-**bon**) trombone 43

la **trompa** (la **trom**-pa) French horn 43

la **trompeta** (la trom-**peh**-ta) trumpet 43

el **trompo** (el **trom**-po) top 35

la **trona** (la **tro**-na) high chair 8

tropezar (tro-peh-**sar**) to stumble 64

la **tuba** (la **too**-ba) tuba 43

las **tumbas** (las **toom**-bas) graves 41

el **túnel de gateo** (el **too**-nel deh ga-**teh**-o) crawling tunnel 31

el **turbante** (el toor-**ban**-teh) turban 73

el **turista** (el too-**rees**-ta) tourist 60

último (**ool**-tee-mo) last 79

el **ultraligero** (el ool-tra-lee-**heh**-ro) ultralight 63

la **uña** (la **oo**-nya) fingernail 19

unir (oo-**neer**) to join 48

uno (**oo**-no) one 33

untar (oon-**tar**) to spread 24

las **uvas** (las **oo**-bas) grapes 11

la **vaca** (la **ba**-ka) cow 45

vacío (ba-**see**-o) empty 26

el **vagón de carga** (el ba-**gon** deh **kar**-go) freight car 61

el **vagón de pasajeros** (el ba-**gon** deh pa-sa-**heh**-ros) passenger car 61

valiente (ba-**lyen**-teh) brave 79

el **vapor** (el ba-**por**) steam 16

el **vaquero** (el ba-**keh**-ro) cowboy 74

la **varita mágica** (la ba-**ree**-ta **ma**-hee-ka) magic wand 41

el **vaso** (el **ba**-so) glass 7

la **vecina** (la beh-**see**-na) neighbor (f.) 7

el **vecino** (el beh-**see**-no) neighbor (m.) 7

la vela (la **beh**-la) candle 7
el velero (el beh-**leh**-ro) sailboat 63
la veleta (la beh-**leh**-ta) weather vane 45
la venda (la **ben**-da) bandage 59
vendar (ben-**dar**) to bandage 65
la ventana (la ben-**ta**-na) window 9
la ventanilla (la ben-ta-**nee**-ya) window 61
ver (ber) to look at 24
el verano (el beh-**ra**-no) summer 32
verde (ber-deh) unripe 66
el verde claro (el **ber**-deh **kla**-ro) light green 30
el verde oscuro (el **ber**-deh os-**koo**-ro) dark green 30
las verduras (las ber-**doo**-ras) vegetables 10
la verja (la **ber**-ha) railings 34
el vestido (el bes-**tee**-doh) dress 22
vestido (bes-**tee**-doh) dressed 27
vestirse (bes-**teer**-seh) to get dressed 25
la vía (la **bee**-a) track 61
viajar (bee-a-**har**) to travel 65
el vídeo (el **bee**-deh-o) video recorder 13
viejo (**byeh**-ho) old 26
el viernes (el **byer**-nehs) Friday 32
la viga (la **bee**-ga) beam 44
vigilar (bee-hee-**lar**) to guard 65
la viola (la bee-**o**-la) viola 42
el violín (el byo-**leen**) violin 42
el violonchelo (el byo-lon-**seh**-lo) cello 42
virar (bee-**rar**) to turn 65
la vitrina (la bee-**tree**-na) display cabinet 15
volar (bo-**lar**) to fly 76
el voleibol (el bo-leh-**bol**) volleyball 38
la voltereta (la bol-teh-**reh**-ta) somersault 37

el walkie-talkie (el **wa**-kee-**ta**-kee) walkie-talkie 54
el windsurf (el **weend**-soorf) windsurfing 39

el xilofón (el see-lo-**fon**) xylophone 42

el yate (el **ya**-teh) yacht 63
la yegua (la **yeh**-gwa) mare 44

el yeso (el **yeh**-so) cast 59
el yogur (el yo-**goor**) yogurt 9
el yoyó (el yo-**yo**) yo-yo 35

el zafacón (el sa-fa-**kon**) garbage can 9
la zanahoria (la sa-na-**o**-rya) carrot 10
las zapatillas (las sa-pa-**tee**-yas) sneakers 23
los zapatos (los sa-**pa**-tohs) shoes 23
los zapatos de tenis (los sa-**pa**-tohs deh **teh**-nees) sneakers 36

PHRASES

Buenos días. ¿Cómo te llamas? (**bweh**-nos dee-yas. **ko**-mo teh **ya**-mas?) 80
Me llamo Ana. (meh **ya**-mo **a**-na) 80
Buenas tardes. ¿Cómo estás? (**bweh**-nas **tar**-dehs. **ko**-mo es-**tas**?) 80
Estoy muy bien, gracias. (es-**toy** mooy byen **gra**-syas) 80
¿Cuántos años tiene el bebé? (**kwan**-tohs a-nyos **tyeh**-neh el beh-**beh**?) 80
Él tiene un año. ¡Feliz cumpleaños! (el **tyeh**-neh oon **a**-nyo. feh-**lees** koom-pleh-**a**-nyos!) 80
¿Cuál es la fecha? (kwal es la **feh**-cha?) 80
Hoy es el cuatro de Julio. (oy es el **kwa**-tro deh **hoo**-lyo) 80
¡Tengo frío! (**ten**-go **free**-o!) 80
Estoy enfermo. (es-**toy** en-**fer**-mo) 80
Elena tiene sed. (eh-**len**-a **tyeh**-nay sed) 80
Tengo miedo. (**ten**-go **myeh**-do) 80
¿Tienes calor? (**tyeh**-nehs ka-**lor**?) 81
No, tengo sueño. (no **ten**-go **sweh**-nyo) 81
¿Cómo está Cristina? (**ko**-mo es-**ta** kree-**stee**-na?) 81
Ella está triste. (**eh**-ya es-**ta trees**-teh) 81

Las hermanas están contentas. (lahs er-**ma**-nas es-**tan** kon-**ten**-tas) 81
Los amigos están contentos también. (los ah-**mee**-gos es-**tan** kon-**ten**-tos tam-**byen**) 81
Hace sol. (a-seh sol) 81
Está lloviendo. ¡Hasta la vista! (es-**ta** yo-**byen**-do. **ahs**-ta la **bees**-ta) 81
¿Qué llevas? (keh **yeh**-bas?) 81
Llevo los zapatos. (**yeh**-bo los sa-**pa**-tohs) 81
¿Qué color es tu falda? (keh ko-**lor** es too **fal**-da?) 81
Mi falda es morada. (mee **fal**-da es mo-**ra**-da) 81
¿Qué hace Maria? (keh **a**-seh Ma-**ree**-a?) 81
Ella salta la cuerda. (**eh**-ya **sal**-ta la **kwer**-da) 81
¿Qué haces, Jorge? (keh **a**-sehs **hor**-heh?) 82
Tiro el balón. (**tee**-ro el ba-**lon**) 82
¿Qué hace Roberto? (keh **a**-seh ro-**ber**-toh?) 82
Él come por que tiene hambre. (el **ko**-meh por keh **tyeh**-neh **am**-breh) 82
¿Quién besa al muchacho? (kyen **beh**-sa al moo-**cha**-cho?) 82
La muchacha besa al muchacho. (lah moo-**cha**-cha **beh**-sa al moo-**cha**-cho) 82
¿Quién tiene el libro? (kyen **tyeh**-neh el **lee**-bro?) 82
La profesora tiene el libro. (la pro-feh-**so**-ra **tyeh**-neh el **lee**-bro) 82
¿Donde estás? (**don**-deh es-**tas**?) 82
Estoy dentro de la casa. (es-**toy** **den**-tro deh la **ka**-sa) 82
Mira a la derecha. Mira a la izquierda. (**mee**-ra a la deh-**reh**-cha. **mee**-ra a la ees-**kyer**-da) 82
Y ahora cruza la calle. (ee ah-**or**-a **kroo**-sa la **ka**-yeh) 82
Aquí viene el autobús. ¿Adónde vas? (ah-**kee byeh**-neh el ow-toh-**boos**. ah-**dohn**-deh bahs?) 82
Voy a la escuela. (boy a la es-**kweh**-lah) 82
¿Qué vas a hacer? (keh bas ah **a**-ser?) 82
Voy a jugar al fútbol. (boy a hoo-**gar** al **foot**-bol) 82

ENGLISH-SPANISH GLOSSARY

accordion el acordeón 43
air el aire 63
air bed la colchoneta 68
alarm clock el despertador 21
album el álbum 35
alcohol el alcohol 58
alike iguales 79
almonds las almendras 10
alphabet el abecedario 31
ambulance la ambulancia 62
angel el ángel 75
animals los animales 46
ankle el tobillo 18
ants las hormigas 71
apple la manzana 11
apricot el albaricoque 11
April abril 32
apron el delantal 56
arm el brazo 18
armchair la butaca, el sillón 14
armoire el armario 15
around alrededor 51
artichoke la alcachofa 10
asleep dormido 27
asparagus, green los espárragos trigueros 10
asparagus, white los espárragos blancos 10
astronaut el astronauta 74
ATM el cajero automático 53
to attack atacar 77
attentive atenta 50
August agosto 32
aunt la tía 7
autumn/fall el otoño 32
avocado el aguacate 11
awake despierto 27
awning el toldo 53
axe el hacha 45

baby el bebé 6
back la espalda 19
backpack la mochila 28
bad-mannered maleducada 79
bag la bolsa 6
balconies los balcones 52
ball la pelota 21; el ovillo 29; el balón 34;
   la bola 41
ballet dancer la bailarina 74
balloons los globos 6
banana la banana 11
bandage la venda 59
to bandage vendar 65
Band-Aid la tirita 58
banister la barandilla 35
banjo el banjo 42
bank el banco 53
banner el banderín 57
bar la barra 9
bar code el código de barras 57
barbecue la barbacoa 70
barefoot descalzo 27
barn el establo 44
barrel el barril 45
barrette la horquilla 35
barrier la barrera 61
baseball el béisbol 38
basket la canasta 34; la cesta 57

basketball el baloncesto 38
bassoon el bajón 43
bat el murciélago 41
bath la bañera 16
bathrobe la bata 16
bathroom el cuarto de baño 16
bathrooms los servicios 59
beach la playa 68
beach umbrella la sombrilla 68
beam la viga 44
beans las judías verdes 10
bear, brown el oso pardo 47
beard la barba 40
bed la cama 15
bedroom el dormitorio 20
bedspread la colcha 20
bee la abeja 70
beehive el panal 70
behind detrás 51
bell el cencerro 45; el cascabel 72
belly button el ombligo 18
bench el banco 52
between entre 51
bib el babero 8
bicycle la bicicleta 54
bidet el bidé 16
big grande 26
binder el álbum 29
binoculars los prismáticos 61
birds los pájaros 70
bitter amargo 66
black el negro 30
blackboard la pizarra 29
blanket la manta 20
blender la batidora 9
blinds la persiana 12
to blow soplar 24
to blow one's nose soplarse la nariz 65
blue, dark el azul oscuro 30
blue, light el azul claro 30
boat la barca 69
body el cuerpo 18
bolt of lightning el rayo 41
bone el hueso 71
book el libro 13
bookcase el librero 15
boots las botas 23
bored aburrida 67
bottle la botella 7; el biberón 21
to bounce botar 49
bowl el tazón 8
bowling los bolos 55
boy el niño 29
bracelet la pulsera 35
braids las trenzas 35
to brake frenar 65
branch la rama 70
brave valiente 79
to break partir 24
to break up picar 77
breakdown la avería 52
breast/chest el pecho 18
to breathe respirar 65
bridge el puente 68
broom el cepillo 12; la escoba 41
brother el hermano 6
brown el marrón 30

to brush cepillar 25
bubble la bomba 73
bucket el cubo 69
to build construir 76
bull el toro 45
bull's-eye la diana 73
bumper el parachoques 53
bunch of flowers el ramo de flores 70
bungee jumping el puenting 39
bunny el gazapo 44
bus el autobús 62
bus stop la parada de autobús 52
busy ocupado 67
butcher el carnicero 56
butcher's la carnicería 56
butterfly la mariposa 71
button el botón 21
to button abrochar 49
buttoned abrochado 26
buttonhole el ojal 21

cactus el cactus 13
cake la torta 6
cakes los pasteles 53
calf la pantorrilla 19; el ternero 45
calm tranquila 67
camcorder la cámara de vídeo 61
camel el camello 47
camera la cámara de fotos 60
to camp acampar 76
camping la acampada 70
candle la vela 7
candleholder el candelabro 12
candlesticks las palmatorias 72
candy cane el bastón de caramelo 73
canned food las conservas 57
canoe la canoa 63
canoeing el piragüismo 39
cap la gorra 69
car el carro 62; el coche 53; el cochecito 55
cardigan la chaqueta 22
cards las cartas 34
carrot la zanahoria 10
cart el carrito de equipaje 61
carton el cartón 8
case el estuche 28
cash register la caja registradora 55
cashew nuts los anacardos 10
cashier la cajera 57
casserole la cazuela 9
cast el yeso 59
castanets las castañuelas 42
castle el castillo 68
cat el gato 72
caterpillar la oruga 71
caught atrapada 78
cavewoman la mujer prehistórica 75
CD el CD 13
ceiling el techo 12
cello el violonchelo 42
cemetery el cementerio 41
cereal los cereales 8
chain la cadena 41
chair la silla 14
chard la acelgas 10
checkers las damas 55

cherry la cereza 7
chess el ajedrez 55
chicks los pollos 44
chimney la chimenea 45
chimpanzee el chimpancé 47
chin la barbilla 19
Chinese box la caja china 42
to chop down talar 77
church la iglesia 52
circle el círculo 30, 35
clarinet el clarinete 43
clean limpia 27
to clean limpiar 25
cleaner la limpiadora 60
cleaner's cart el carro de limpieza 60
clay la plastilina 29
to climb escalar 77
climbing la escalada 39
clock el reloj 6
to close cerrar 64
closed cerrado 26, 66
cloth el trapo 12
clothes la ropa 22
clothes rack el perchero 28
cloud la nube 68
cloudy nublado 78
clown el pehaso 72
club la maza 36
coat el abrigo 23
coconut el coco 11
coffeemaker la cafetera 9
coin purse la carterita 57
coins las monedas 57
cold frío 26
collector el revisor 60
cologne la colonia 16
to color colorear 48
colors los colores 30
comb el peine 17
to comb one's hair peinarse 25
combed peinado 27
comfortable cómoda 27
comforter el edredón 20
comic la tira cómica 35
compass la brújula 71
computer la computadora 13
conga drums las congas 42
container el contenedor 57
convertible el descapotable 68
cook la cocinera 74
to cook cocinar 24
cookies las galletas 35
corner la esquina 12
cornet la corneta 43
costumes los disfraces 74
cotton el algodón 59
cotton candy el algodón de azúcar 73
cotton swabs los bastoncillos 17
to cough toser 65
to count contar 48
counter el mostrador 56
couple la pareja 73
cousin el primo 7
cow la vaca 45
coward cobarde 79
cowboy el vaquero 74
crab el cangrejo 69
to crash chocarse 65
crawling tunnel el túnel de gateo 36
crib la cuna 15, 20
crooked torcido 26
crops los cultivos 70
to cross cruzar 64
to cross out tachar 48
crown la corona 7
crumbs las migas 52

crutch la muleta 35
to cry llorar 65
crystal ball la bola de cristal 72
cube el cubo 37
cup la taza 9
to cure curar 65
curious curioso 67
curly rizado 50
curtain la cortina 9; el telón 41
cushion el cojín 12
cut partido 66
to cut cortar 48
to cut one's nails cortarse las uñas 25
cutting board la tabla para cortar 8
cycling el ciclismo 38
cymbals los crótalos 41

dart el dardo 73
days los días 32
December diciembre 32
deck chair la silla de playa 68
deflated desinflado 78
deodorant el desodorante 17
desk la mesa de despacho 14; el escritorio 15
devil el diablo 75
diaper el pañal 20
different distintos 79
difficult difícil 78
to dig cavar 77
dining table la mesa de comedor 14
dinosaur el dinosaurio 21
dirty sucia 27
dishwasher el lavaplatos 9
display cabinet la vitrina 15
distracted distraída 50
divan el diván 14
to dive bucear 76
doctor la doctora 58
dog el perro 45
doll el muñeco 21; la muñeca 55
domestic doméstico 79
dominoes el dominó 54
donkey el burro 45
door la puerta 12
double bass el contrabajo 42
doughnut la rosquilla 7
down abajo 51
to drag arrastrar 49
dragon el dragón 40
dragonfly la libélula 71
drain la alcantarilla 52
to draw dibujar 48
drawer el cajón 21
drawings los dibujos 29
dress el vestido 22
dressed vestido 27
dresser la cómoda 15
dressing table el tocador 15
drill el taladro 13
to drink beber 24
drinking straw el pitillo 6
to drive conducir 64
driver la conductora 53
dromedary el dromedario 47
drum el tambor 42
drum set la batería 42
dry seca 27
to dry oneself secarse 25
duck el pato 44
dustpan el recogedor 13

ear la oreja 19
easel el caballete 29

easy fácil 78
to eat comer 24
eight ocho 33
eighth octava 33
elbow el codo 19
electric guitar la guitarra eléctrica 42
electronic game el juego electrónico 55
elephant el elefante 46
elf el duende 41
empty vacío 26
engine driver el conductor 60
to erase borrar 48
eraser el borrador 29; la goma 29
excavator la excavadora 62
exit la salida 40
to explain explicar 48
eyebrow la ceja 19
eyelashes las pestañas 19
eyelid el párpado 19
eyes los ojos 19

fairy el hada 40
family la familia 6
far lejos 51
farm la granja 44
farmer el granjero 44
fast rápida 78
fat gordo 50
father el padre 6
faucet el grifo 17
feather la pluma 41
feather duster el plumero 13
February febrero 32
fence la cerca 70
fencing la esgrima 39
Ferris wheel la noria 72
fierce feroz 79
fifth quinta 33
fingernail la uña 19
fingers los dedos 19
fire engine el carro de bomberos 62
fire escape la escalera de incendios 53
fire extinguisher el extintor 37
fireman el bombero 74
firewood la leña 45
first primera 33, 79
fish el pescado 56; el pez 70
to fish pescar 77
fisherman el pescador 71
fishing rod la caña de pescar 71
fishmonger la pescadera 56
five cinco 33
flag la bandera 53
flashlight la linterna 41
flip-flops las chanclas 68
to float flotar 76
floats los manguitos 69
flock of sheep el rebaño 71
flowerpot la maceta 35
fluorescent light el fluorescente 37
flute la flauta travesera 43
to fly volar 76
folded doblado 78
folder la carpeta 21
folding chair la silla plegable 68
foot el pie 18
footprints las huellas 68
forearm el antebrazo 19
forehead la frente 19
fork el tenedor 9
fortune-teller la adivina 72
four cuatro 33
fourth cuarto 33

fragile frágil 78
frame el marco 12
free libre 67, 78
freight car el vagón de carga 61
French horn la trompa 43
Friday el viernes 32
fridge la nevera 9
fried fritas 66
from desde 51
frozen food los congelados 57
fruit los frutos 10; la fruta 56
fruit stall la frutería 56
fryer la freidora 9
frying pan el sartén 9
full lleno 26
furniture los muebles 14

games los juegos 54
garbage can el zafacón 9
gardener el jardinero 34
garlic el ajo 10
gas pump el surtidor 68
gas station la gasolinera 68
gauze bandage la gasa 58
to get dirty mancharse 25
to get dressed vestirse 25
to get up levantarse 25
ghost el fantasma 40
giraffe la jirafa 46
girl la niña 29
to give a present regalar 24
glass el vaso 7
glasses las gafas 35
gloves los guantes 57
glue la pega 29
to glue pegar 48
to go to bed acostarse 25
to go down bajar 64
to go in entrar 64
to go out salir 64
to go up subir 64
goal la portería 34
goalie el portero 34
goat la cabra 44
goatee la perilla 40
goggles las gafas de bucear 69
golf el golf 38
good-looking guapo 50
goose la oca 45
gorilla el gorila 47
grandfather el abuelo 6
grandmother la abuela 6
grapefruit la toronja 11
grapes las uvas 11
grass la hierba 71
graves las tumbas 41
gray el gris 30
greedy golosa 67
green, dark el verde oscuro 30
green, light el verde claro 30
to greet saludar 49
to guard vigilar 65
guitar la guitarra 42
gym el gimnasio 36

hairbrush el cepillo 17
hair dryer el secador 17
half moon la medialuna 30
hamburger la hamburguesa 73
hammer el martillo 13
hammock la hamaca 70
hand la mano 18
handball el balonmano 38
handbell la campanilla 40

to hang up tender 25
hanger el gancho 21
hang gliding el ala delta 39
happy contento 27
hard duro 67
harmonica la armónica 43
hat el gorro 23, 57
hayloft el pajar 45
hazelnuts las avellanas 10
head la cabeza 19
headband la diadema 35
healthy sano 67
heart el corazón 30, 58
heel el talón 19
helicopter el helicóptero 63
helmet el casco 53
hens las gallinas 44
to hide esconderse 49
hide-and-seek el escondite 34
high chair la trona 8
high jump el salto de altura 39
hiking el montañismo 39
hippopotamus el hipopótamo 46
hockey el hockey 38
hoe la azada 45
to hold sujetar 49
hole el hoyo 68
hoop el aro 37
horse el caballo 44
horseback riding la hípica 38
hose la manguera 34
hot caliente 26
hot dog el perrito caliente 73
hot-air balloon el globo 63
hotel el hotel 52
housecoat la bata 21
to hug abrazar 24
hurdle jump el salto de vallas 39
hutch la alacena 15

ice el hielo 7
ice-cream cone la barquilla 69
ice-cream pop el polo 69
in dentro 51
in front of delante 51
index finger el índice 19
industrious trabajador 67
inflatable castle el castillo hinchable 72
inflated inflado 78
information board el panel de información 60
information desk la información 60
injury la herida 58
inner tube el flotador 69
iron la plancha 13
to iron planchar 25
ironed estirada 26
ironing board la tabla de planchar 12
island la isla 69

jam la mermelada 9
January enero 32
jars los frascos 8; los botes 29
jean jacket la chaqueta 23
jester el bufón 75
jet ski la moto acuática 68
jigsaw puzzle el rompecabezas 54
to join unir 48
juggler el malabarista 72
juice el jugo 8
juicer el exprimidor 9
July julio 32
to jump saltar 49

jump rope la comba 34
jumper el pichi 22
June junio 32

kangaroo el canguro 47
kettle drum el timbal 42
key la llave 13
key ring el llavero 13
keyboard el teclado 13
keyboard instruments los instrumentos con teclado 43
to kick dar una patada 49
king el rey 75
kiosk el quiosco 68
to kiss besar 24
kitchen la cocina 8
kite la cometa 68
kiwi el kiwi 11
knee la rodilla 19
knee pad la rodillera 36
knife el cuchillo 9
knight el caballero 75
knitted shirt el polo 22
knob el tirador 17
knuckles los nudillos 19
koala el koala 47

laces los cordones 21
ladder la escalera 20
ladybug la mariquita 71
lake el lago 71
lamp la lámpara 12
lamppost el farol 53
land la tierra 62
to land aterrizar 64
landscape el paisaje 12
last último 79
to laugh reír 65
laundry basket la cesta 12
lazy perezoso 67
leaves las hojas 70
leek el puerro 10
leg la pierna 18
Lego bricks las construcciones 54
lemon el limón 11
leopard el leopardo 46
leotard la malla 36
to let go of soltar 49
letters las letras 28
lettuce la lechuga 10
license plate la matrícula 53
to lick chupar 77; lamer 77
lid la tapa 8
life jacket el chaleco salvavidas 69
lifeguard el salvavidas 68
to light alumbrar 65
light aircraft la avioneta 63
lighthouse el faro 69
line la fila 34
lion el león 46
lips los labios 19
lipstick el pintalabios 17
liquid líquido 66
to listen oír 24; escuchar 48
living room el cuarto de estar 12
lizard la lagartija 71
llama la llama 46
to load cargar 65
long largo 50
long jump el salto de longitud 39
to look at ver 24
loudspeakers los altavoces 60
luggage la consigna 61
lung el pulmón 58

lying recostada 50
lynx el lince 46

magic wand la varita mágica 41
magician el mago 72
magnet el imán 9
magnifying glass la lupa 70
mail carrier el cartero 53
mailbox el buzón 53
to make one's bed hacer la cama 25
to make up maquillar 49
mane los crines 44
mango el mango 11
map el mapa 28
maracas las maracas 42
marbles las canicas 34
March marzo 32
mare la yegua 44
marker el rotulador 29
maroon el granate 30
martial arts las artes marciales 39
mask la careta 7, 72; la mascarilla 58
mat la colchoneta 36
matches los fósforos 7
mattress el colchón 20
May mayo 32
means los medios 62
meat la carne 56
mechanic la mecánica 74
medal la medalla 35
medical tape el esparadrapo 58
medicine las medicinas 58
medicine cabinet el botiquín 16
medlar el níspero 11
melon el melón 11
to melt derretirse 76
memorial el monumento 52
merry-go-round el tiovivo 72
messy desordenado 26
microphone el micrófono 73
microwave el microondas 8
middle finger el del corazón 19
mirror el espejo 17
mittens las manoplas 57
mobile phone el celular 53
modern moderno 66
molars las muelas 19
mold el molde 69
Monday el lunes 32
monster el monstruo 40
months los meses 32
moon la luna 40
to mop trapear 25
mother la madre 6
motorcycle la moto 62
mountain la montaña 70
mouse el ratón 13, 75
mousepad la alfombrilla 13
moustache el bigote 40
mouth la boca 19
movie theater el cine 52
to mow segar 77
muscles los músculos 58
mushroom la seta 40
musical instruments los instrumentos
    musicales 42
musketeer el mosquetero 75

to nail clavar 77
nailbrush el cepillo de uñas 17
nails los clavos 13
napkin la servilleta 6
narrow estrecho 78
near cerca 51

neat ordenado 26
neck el cuello 19
necklace el collar 35
neighbor la vecina (f.) 7; el vecino (m.)
    7
nervous nerviosa 67
nest el nido 71
new nuevo 26
newspaper el periódico 61
next to al lado de 51
nightgown el camisón 21
nightstand la mesilla 21
nine nueve 33
ninth noveno 33
noisemaker el matasuegras 7
normal normal 79
nose la nariz 19
November noviembre 32
numbers los números 33
nurse la enfermera 58

oboe el oboe 43
ochre el ocre 30
October octubre 32
off apagada 26
office la oficina 58
ointment la pomada 59
old viejo 26; anciano 50; antiguo 66
on encendida 26; encima 51
one uno 33
onion la cebolla 10
open abierto 26, 66
to open abrir 64
opposite enfrente 51
optician's la óptica 53
orange (color) el naranja 30
orange (fruit) la naranja 11
orangutan el orangután 47
organ el órgano 43
ottoman el banquillo 14
out fuera 51
oval el óvalo 30
oven el horno 8
overalls el pantalón de peto 23

pacifier el chupete 21
to paint pintar 77
paintbrush el pincel 29
painter el pintor 74
paintings los cuadros 12
paints la pinturas 28
pajama el pijama 20
palate el paladar 19
pale pálida 79
panda bear el oso panda 47
panpipes la flauta andina 43
panther la pantera 46
panties las pantaletas 22
pants el pantalón largo 23
paper lantern el farolillo 72
paper streamer la serpentina 6
paper towels el papel de cocina 9
parallel bars las paralelas 37
Parcheesi el parchís 55
park el parque 52
partition la mampara 16
parts las partes 18
to pass adelantar 65
passenger car el vagón de pasajeros 61
path el camino 41
patient el paciente 58
peach el melocotón 11
peanuts los cacauetes 10
pear la pera 11

peas los guisantes 10
pedal boat el patín 69
to peel pelar 24
pen el bolígrafo 29; el redil 44
pencil el lápiz 29
pencil sharpener el sacapuntas 29
penknife la navaja 70
pepper, green el pimiento verde 10
pepper, red el pimiento rojo 10
percussion instruments los instrumentos de
    percusión 42
to perform actuar 49
perfume el perfume 16
to pet acariciar 24
phone booth la cabina telefónica 53
photograph la fotografía 28
photographer la fotógrafa 74
piano el piano 43
pick el pico 61
pictures las fotos 35
pieces of chalk las tizas 28
pig el cerdo 45
pigeons las palomas 52
piggy bank la alcancía 21
piglet el lechón 45
pigsty la pocilga 44
pike la pica 36
pillow la almohada 20
pills las pastillas 59
pincers las tenazas 13
pineapple la piña 11
ping-pong el ping-pong 39
pink el rosa 30
pinky el meñique 19
pipe la cañería 34
pirate el pirata 75
pistachio nuts los pistachos 10
pitcher la jarra 7; la garrafa 70
plane el avión 63
plant la planta 6
plate el plato 9
plate rack el escurreplatos 9
platform el andén 61
to play jugar 48
to play an instrument tocar un instrumento
    48
pliers los alicates 13
to plow arar 77
plug el tapón 17
to point señalar 76
polar bear el oso polar 47
policewoman la policía 74
pond la charca 45
pony el potro 44
ponytail la coleta 34
popcorn las palomitas 73
portrait el retrato 12
post office el correo 52
poster el póster 20
potato la papa 10
potato chips las papas fritas 73
potty el orinal 17
present el regalo 6
prince el príncipe 41
to prune podar 77
puddle el charco 52
puma el puma 46
pumpkin la calabaza 10
puppet la marioneta 73
puppets los títeres 55
puppy el cachorro 45
purple el morado 30
purse el bolso 57
to push empujar 49
to put cream on ponerse crema 76
puzzle el rompecabezas 54

rabbit el conejo 44
race la carrera 39
race car el carro de carreras 62
race driver el piloto 74
racket la raqueta 20
radio el radio 16
radio cassette el radiocasete 21
rafting el rafting 39
rail el raíl 61
railings la verja 34
rainbow el arco iris 69
raincoat el impermeable 23
raisins las pasas 11
rake el rastrillo 45
ram el carnero 44
ramp la rampa 35
range hood la campana extractora 8
rattle el sonajero 21
raw crudas 66
razor el rastrillo 17
to read leer 48
reading lamp el flexo 20
record player el tocadiscos 13
recorder la flauta dulce 43
rectangle el rectángulo 30
red el rojo 30
reins las riendas 45
remote-controlled car el coche teledirigido 21
resistant resistente 78
rhino el rinoceronte 46
ribbon el lazo 35; la cinta 36
to ride a bicycle montar en bicicleta 64
ring la sortija 35
ring finger el anular 19
rings las anillas 37
ripe maduro 66
river el río 70
road la calzada 53
road sign la señal de tráfico 53
robot el robot 20
rocket el cohete 63
rocking chair la mecedora 14
rocking horse el balancín 55
roller blind el estor 6
roller coaster la montaña rusa 72
rolling pin el rodillo 9
rooster el gallo 45
rope la cuerda de nudos 36; la soga 70
rough áspero 66
to row remar 76
rowboat el bote de remos 63
rug la alfombra 13
rugby el rugby 38
ruler la regla 29
to run correr 76

sack el saco 61
sad triste 27
saddle la silla de montar 45
saddlebag las alforjas 45
to sail navegar 76
sailboat el velero 63
saltshaker el salero 7
salty salado 66
sand la arena 69
sandals las sandalias 23
sandwich el sándwich 7
Saturday el sábado 32
saucepan el cazo 8
to saw serrar 77
saxophone el saxofón 43
to say good-bye despedirse 65
scale la báscula 16
scales la balanza 57

scarecrow el espantapájaros 71
scarf la bufanda 57; el pañuelo 57
scientist el científico 74
scissors las tijeras 29
scooter el patinete 54
to scratch arañar 77
screen la pantalla 13
screwdriver el destornillador 13
sea el mar 69
seasons las estaciones 32
seat el asiento 59
seated sentada 50
seats las butacas 40
second segunda 33
to separate separar 48
September septiembre 32
to serve servir 24
seven siete 33
seventh séptimo 33
to sew coser 49
shampoo el champú 16
to shape modelar 48
shapes las formas 30
to sharpen sacar punta 48
to shave afeitarse 25
sheep la oveja 45
sheet la sábana 20
sheet of paper la hoja 28
shell la concha 69
shepherd el pastor 71
shin la espinilla 19
ship el barco 63
shirt la camisa 22
to shiver tiritar 76
shoes los zapatos 23
shoots los brotes 28
shopping cart el carro 57
short baja 50; corto 50
shorts el pantalón corto 23
shoulder el hombro 19
shovel la pala 69
shower la ducha 16
shower gel el gel 16
sick enfermo 67
sideboard el aparador 15
sidewalk la acera 53
sign el cartel 59
singer el cantante 72
sink el fregadero 9; el lavabo 17
to sink hundirse 76
sister la hermana 6
six seis 33
sixth sexta 33
skateboard el monopatín 54
skates los patines 54
skating el patinaje 38
skeleton el esqueleto 72
skiing el esquí 38
skirt la falda 22
skull la calavera 58
to sleep dormir 25
slide la chorrera 52
to slip resbalar 64
to slither reptar 76
slow lenta 78
small pequeño 26
to smell oler 24
smoke el humo 70
snail el caracol 71
snake la serpiente 47
sneakers las zapatillas 23; los zapatos de tenis 36
to sneeze estornudar 65
to sniff oler 77
snow la nieve 70
snowboarding el snowboard 39

soap el jabón 17
soccer el fútbol 38
socket el enchufe 13
socks los calcetines 22
sofa el sofá 14
soft suave 66; blando 67
soft drink el refresco 73
soldier el soldado 75
solid sólido 66
somersault la voltereta 37
sour ácido 66
to sow sembrar 77
spaceship la nave espacial 73
to speak hablar 48
speaker la bocina 13
spectators los espectadores 40
to speed up acelerar 65
speedboat la lancha 63
spice rack el especiero 8
spicy picante 66
spider la araña 71
spider's web la telaraña 71
to splash salpicar 76
spoiled estropeado 66
sponge la esponja 17
spoon la cuchara 9
sports los deportes 38
spotlights los focos 40
spray bottle el rociador 13
to spread untar 24
spring la primavera 32
springboard el trampolín 37
square el cuadrado 30
squatting en cuclillas 50
stable la cuadra 44
stage el escenario 40
standing de pie 50
star la estrella 30
steam el vapor 16
stereo el equipo de música 13
stethoscope el fonendoscopio 59
to sting picar 77
stomach el estómago 58
stone la piedra 70
stool el banco 16
stopwatch el cronómetro 37
store la tienda 52
storybook el cuento 21
straight recto 26; liso 50
strainer el colador 9
strange raro 79
strawberries la fresa 11
to stretch estirarse 25
stretched estirado 78
stretcher la camilla 58
string instruments los instrumentos de cuerda 42
to stroll pasear 64
stroller la sillita 57
strong fuerte 50
students los alumnos 28
to stumble tropezar 64
subway el metro 53
to suckle mamar 77
sugar bowl el azucarero 9
suitcase la maleta 60
sultan el sultán 75
summer el verano 32
sun el sol 68
to sunbathe tomar el sol 76
Sunday el domingo 32
sunglasses las gafas de sol 69
sunny soleado 78
sunscreen la crema protectora 69
superhero el superhéroe 75
supermarket el supermercado 56

95

surgical collar el collarín 73
sweat el sudor 36
to sweat sudar 49
sweater el jersey 22
to sweep barrer 25
sweet dulce 66
swimming la natación 38
swimming trunks el traje de baño de niño 23
swimsuit el traje de baño de niña 23
switch el interruptor 13
sword la espada 41
syringe la jeringuilla 59
syrup el jarabe 59

table, round la mesa camilla 14
tablecloth el mantel 6
to take a bath bañarse 25
to take a shower ducharse 76
to take off despegar 64
talcum powder el polvo de talco 17
to talk on the phone hablar por teléfono 64
tall alta 50
tambourine la pandereta 41, 42
tame manso 79
tan morena 79
tape el papel celo 29
target shooting el tiro al blanco 73
tassels los flecos 13
to taste gustar 24
taxi el taxi 62
teacher la profesora 28
teaspoon la cucharilla 9
teddy bear el oso de peluche 54
teeth los dientes 19
television el televisor 12
ten diez 33
tennis el tenis 38
tent la tienda de campaña 70
tenth décimo 33
theater el teatro 40
thermometer el termómetro 59
thermos el termo 71
thick gruesa 66
thigh el muslo 19
thin delgado 50; fina 66
third tercero 33
three tres 33
through a través de 51
to throw tirar 49
thumb el pulgar 19
Thursday el jueves 32
to tie up atar 49
tiger el tigre 46
tights los leotardos 22
tiles las baldosas 16
time el tiempo 32
tire la llanta 53
tired cansada 50
tissues los pañuelos de papel 17
to hasta 51
toad el sapo 45
toast la tostada 8
toaster la tostadora 9
toilet el inodoro 16
toilet paper el papel higiénico 16
tomato el tomate 10
tongue la lengua 19
toolbox la caja de herramientas 13
toothbrush el cepillo de dientes 17
toothpaste la pasta de dientes 17
toothpicks los palillos 7
top el trompo 35
top hat el sombrero de copa 73
tortoise la tortuga 47

to touch tocar 24
tourist el turista 60
toward hacia 51
towel la toalla 17
tower la torre 68
town el pueblo 70
toys los juguetes 54
track la vía 61
tracksuit el chándal 36
tractor el tractor 62
traffic light el semáforo 53
trailer el carromato 72
train el tren 62
train station la estación de tren 60
trampoline la cama elástica 37
transportation el transporte 62
to travel viajar 65
tray la bandeja 8
treasure el tesoro 40
tree el árbol 71
triangle el triángulo 30, 41
tricycle el triciclo 54
trip la excursión 44
trombone el trombón 43
trough el pesebre 44
truck el camión 62
trumpet la trompeta 43
trunk el baúl 20
T-shirt la camiseta 22
tuba la tuba 43
Tuesday el martes 32
turban el turbante 73
turkey el pavo 45
to turn virar 65
to turn somersaults dar una voltereta 49
turnip el nabo 10
twig el palo 70
two dos 33

ugly feo 50
ultralight el ultraligero 63
umbrella el paraguas 61
to unbutton desabrochar 49
uncle el tío 6
unbuttoned desabrochado 26
uncombed despeinado 27
uncomfortable incómoda 27
under debajo 51
underpants los calzoncillos 22
undressed desvestido 27
to unload descargar 65
unripe verde 66
to untie desatar 49
to unwrap desenvolver 48
up arriba 51
usher la acomodadora 40
uvula la campanilla 19

vacuum la aspiradora 12
van la camioneta 62
vase el jarrón 12
vaulting box el plinto 37
vaulting horse el potro 37
vegetables las verduras 10
vest el chaleco 22
video recorder el vídeo 13
viola la viola 42
violin el violín 42
volleyball el voleibol 38

waist la cintura 19
to wait esperar 64

waiting room la sala de espera 59
to walk andar 76
walkie-talkie el walkie-talkie 54
walking stick el bastón 40
wall la pared 13
wall bars las espalderas 36
wallet la billetera 57
walnuts las nueces 11
to wash lavar los platos 24
to wash oneself lavarse 25
washing machine la lavadora 9
wastepaper bin la papelera 29
to watch observar 76
watch el reloj de pulsera 37
to water regar 76
water el agua 34
water bottle la cantimplora 71
water fountain la fuente 34
water heater el calentador 9
watercolors las acuarelas 28
watering can la regadera 69
watermelon la sandía 11
wave la ola 69
weak débil 50
weather vane la veleta 45
Wednesday el miércoles 32
week la semana 32
to weigh pesar 65
well-mannered educada 79
wet mojada 27
wheel la rueda 53
wheelbarrow la carretilla 61
wheelchair la silla de ruedas 34
to whisk batir 24
whistle el silbato 35
white el blanco 30
whole entero 66
wide ancho 78
wig la peluca 72
wild salvaje 79
wind instruments los instrumentos de viento 43
windmill el molino 44
window la ventana 9; la ventanilla 61
window box la jardinera 35
window ladder la escala 36
windsurfing el windsurf 39
winter el invierno 32
witch la bruja 41
with a cold acatarrado 67
with shoes on calzado 27
with the lid off destapado 67
with the lid on tapado 67
worker el obrero 61
to wrap envolver 48
wrinkled arrugada 26
wrist la muñeca 19
to write escribir 48

x-ray la radiografía 58
xylophone el xilofón 42

yacht el yate 63
to yawn bostezar 25
yellow el amarillo 30
yogurt el yogur 9
young joven 50
yo-yo el yoyó 35

zebra la cebra 46
zipper la cremallera 21
zucchini el calabacín 10